Strange Nights, and Some Days Too

Why You'll Love Japan, for About a Year

Ken Seeroi

The stories in *Strange Nights, and Some Days Too* are based upon real-life events. Some names and identifying details have been changed.

ISBN: 978-1-7351746-2-4
Shioyaki Press

Second Edition
4 6 8 10 9 7 5

To my mother, father, and brother; the kindest, funniest, and most loving people I know.

Contents

The end of this book contains definitions of the Japanese terms used within.

Hello Tokyo

My first night in Japan was spent in a hotel without a shower or closet, in a silent corner of Tokyo called Nihonbashi. I was like, Where's all the nightlife? I thought this place was supposed to be a parade of colorful bars, bustling restaurants, and busty girls in short skirts? Strange. Instead, I meandered in the dark past the occasional Chinese hooker and wondered if the apocalypse had happened and I'd simply overslept. That'd be just like me. Everyone's gone up to heaven and I missed it 'cause I had a bunch of cocktails on the plane. But eventually I found what appeared to be a local restaurant or possibly just someone's kitchen, slid open the door, and a roomful of Japanese folks suddenly stopped talking and stared in my direction like I was a giant white rabbit. I was like, Surprise! Here's your Easter eggs.

The elderly lady behind the counter and I attempted a conversation, but we were soon reduced to gestures, clicks, and whistles before I managed to get a beer and something to eat. I made do with two pints of Asahi and a soggy grilled eggplant topped with fish food, then left before things got any weirder. On the way back, I stopped at a 7-Eleven, bought a bottle of sake, two rice balls, a bag of shrimp-flavored chips, and a can of habanero soup, then scarfed everything down in my tiny hotel room while watching sumo on TV. I then proceeded downstairs to the communal bath, took off all my clothes and hopped in the tub with a bunch of wrinkly old Japanese dudes who'd apparently left their teeth in the locker room. Well, details aside, I was still naked and drunk in Tokyo, which I count as a win. Such is my optimism.

The next day I ventured out for a couple sobering cocktails, then a couple more, until I bumped into an amazingly beautiful girl named Ran who insisted I check out of my hotel, stuff my suitcases into a locker near the station, and go clubbing with her in Roppongi. Finally some neon. Now that was the Japan I'd come to see. Ran took me to a dinner of

1

udon noodles, followed by a round of karaoke, during which she confessed that she was actually a Victoria's Secret model, which was totally credible. She was stunning, Japan was perfect, and Japanese people were all so friendly. Somehow I ended up paying for everything, but I'm pretty sure that was an oversight. Ran of course later turned out to be a Filipino prostitute, and Roppongi a jumble of grimy bars packed with German tourists and sidewalks full of Nigerian touts pulling me endlessly into hostess bars for drinks with Russian women. So international, Japan. Anyway, I'm just glad I got to have a night of expensive sex I don't remember with a Victoria's Secret model. I woke up the next morning in an unfamiliar room with the hotel manager calling me on the phone to say things I didn't understand and Ran had mysteriously, well, run. I assume she had a photo shoot. Models.

From the day I arrived in Japan, I began studying Japanese. And you know how you look back on your life at things you did when you were younger and you're glad you put the effort into them? Well, Japanese isn't one of 'em. If you want a magic key that opens doors and helps you make friends in the nation, uh, that'd be English.

Moving on. After my Roppongi adventure, I flew back to Japan for a couple weeks every year, before finally settling here in 2008. I've had a score of jobs and girlfriends at this point, some of them good, and some bad. Well, most were pretty horrible, actually. I mean the jobs, of course. The women, well, we'll get to that in a bit. As for making a living, suffice to say Japan isn't known for its easygoing work environment. I've made the yen equivalent of hundreds of dollars an hour (good), and other times got paid nothing more than beer and rice (slightly less good). What can I say, it's a pretty bipolar country. But maybe that's why I feel so at home.

Over the years, I've read everything I could get my hands on about Japan, the people, its culture, and language. You've probably read much of the same stuff. There's a tendency to either glamorize the nation or treat it with cartoonish

Orientalism, and along the way lose sight of the fact that it's a real place populated with real, albeit slightly twisted, people.

It's not easy to depict an entire nation in a few words, and I don't pretend to do so. Well hey, Japan's a big country. But maybe that's the point. It's not something that's summed up easily. Even living here, I barely know what the hell's going on half the time. Actually, half may be generous, but I'll just give you my perspective, for what it's worth. As the Japanese say, Hope you enjoy.

After the Last Train, it's Ramen, Amen

So somehow it came to pass that I found myself in Ikebukuro at 3:30 a.m., drinking malt liquor, eating kimchee and a really fabulous grilled mackerel, helping this random *izakaya* owner translate his signs into English. If you wander into a place there with a hand-written poster reading "A customer must pay when it orders," then yeah, that was me.

Though I'm happy to finally be teaching English in Japan, I'm certain juggling monkeys would be more relaxing. Students rush in and out of my classroom while I madly prepare for the next lesson and remember I left my teaching materials in the men's room stall. On an average day, I teach seven classes, plus give tests, do interviews, and carry out the garbage. I have neither desk nor chair, which is fine, since I'd never be able to sit anyway.

My first week here was spent on the outskirts of Tokyo, in "training." This consisted of random white guys reading all the rules in the company handbook, while overlooking anything about how to actually teach classes. One thing the trainers were clear on was the fast pace of *eikaiwa* life. One guy suggested pursuing hobbies as a way of relieving stress. His hobby: doll collecting.

Since I'm generally receptive to advice, I decided that instead of building a collection of mini people like that weirdo, I'd simply put more effort into my existing hobbies, namely drinking and womanizing. Thus began a steady regimen of hobbying that has grown in force like a tornado to include boozing and making out with teachers, students, and various other unsavory remnants of Tokyo's nightlife. Now, due to circumstances almost beyond my control, I seem to regularly miss the last train and wind up in some dingy ramen shop, staring into the salty broth and wondering why on earth it's come to this. My existence has been reduced to a blur of classes, seeking sustenance, buying clean underwear from convenience stores, and booze.

As I step over a pile of Japanese guys in suits passed out in a doorway, I realize I've lost the ability to distinguish day from night. Right from wrong of course went by the wayside long ago. I still haven't gotten a bank account, cell phone, or the internet, nor have I figured out how to even take out the trash at my apartment, and plus my washing machine freaking exploded this morning and blew water all over the balcony. My fridge is as barren as Antarctica. I'm vaguely aware of working nine or ten hours a day and commuting another two. If it weren't for sleeping on trains, corn soup from vending machines, and my steely resolve, I'd surely perish. At least there are only twelve more months to go, right? And now the staff at this net café are saying something in my direction. Jeezus. I'll just pretend to be dead and maybe they'll leave me alone. If anybody asks, I'm not here.

The Dangers of Japanese Recycling

Thus far I've succeeded in taking out two of my four types of garbage. Trash is so fascinating to Japanese folks that they've seen fit to divide it into four types and given each its own special day of the week for pick-up. There's Plastic Bottle Day, Can Day, Unburnable Trash Day, and Burnable Trash Day. They even have signs printed in English explaining the concepts. And the first time I read the sign, I was like, "burnable?" Man, I've been camping and I know that given a big enough bonfire pretty much anything's burnable. Trust me, I teach English in your country and I know what "burnable" means. Now quit screwing around and let me take out my trash.

Then one fine, gray afternoon, I finally met one of my neighbors in the hall. He was this old Japanese guy, and I saw him as we came out of our respective apartments. So I was like, *konnichiwa*, and he was like, *konnichiwa*. And then he looks at me in fear, like what's the white guy gonna say next? So I leaned in toward him, looked him in the eye, and said in Japanese, "Want some milk?" You can bet he didn't see that coming! Then before he could answer, I ran into my apartment and grabbed a quart. Because, for some kindhearted but misguided reason, one of my co-workers had given me milk and cereal as a welcome gift. As I don't drink milk, I'd been wondering how to get rid of the damn stuff, since it doesn't fit into any known trash category. So I explained this to him and showed him it wasn't expired, and he seemed rather pleased, thanked me, then took his milk and went back to his apartment and locked the door.

And then I had some beer. And because tomorrow is Can Day I figured I'd take out the ever-expanding pile of cans that was threatening to overtake my living quarters. Now, one thing I like about my tiny apartment is that it requires a key to lock, which is good, because it means I can't lock myself out, even while drunk. But one thing I don't like is the feeling I get when I take out the trash and realize it's possible to lock myself out of the entire building.

So I'm outside in my slippers and shorts and no shirt, holding a bag of empty beer cans when I hear the auto-lock click, and I'm like, Ahh...shit, tell me that didn't just happen. Above me, my apartment window is shining bright and cheerily, and I'm standing in the wind all thirsty and have to teach class again in about five hours. I can see people walking by trying to look like they aren't watching me as I test out the drainpipe to see if I can climb it and get up to my place. It's pretty clear at this point that I'm either going to be arrested while scaling the building or plunge to my death trying and wind up shirtless and dead in Tokyo.

And then like a hairy Winnie the Pooh, I sat on the curb and had me a think. But all the while I could feel that ol' dehydrating sobriety setting in, so finally I walked back to the building and rang the intercom and Milk Guy answered. I was like, Remember me? Yeah well, guess what? I'm an idiot and locked myself out, so would you mind? At which point he buzzed me in and I went back to drinking beer in earnest and making more trash for next Can Day. Later that same evening I walked through the sliding screen door to my balcony and sent the screen careening down three floors. Japan has some amazingly transparent door technology. So many close calls. I don't know why people say this country is safe.

Growing Old in Japan

When I finally looked in the mirror after a month of *eikaiwa* teaching, my first thought was—who the hell's that? My signature dark and flowing locks, which had once glowed with the radiance of a dozen hair-care products, had gone white almost overnight. While it's true that I might've had one or two gray hairs before, my class load was clearly making me look like Keith Richards before my time.

Thus, thinking of ways to reverse this trend, I made the rational-while-drunk decision to color things a slightly darker brown. I walked to the 100-yen store in front of the train station and carefully selected the perfect Japanese hair-care product, which when used as directed immediately rendered my hair a vivid Orphan Annie red. So that was bad. But then my buddy Carlos said, That's no problem, just do it again, only leave the dye in longer. And since he's gay, I figured he knew about such things, so that's what I did, only to find that my hair turned a disturbing shade of Concord grape. The following day the Head Teacher at my school pulled me aside to say the Manager was peed off regarding my hair color. I was like, Well I'm not too thrilled about it either, and have taken the matter under consideration.

Every time I tried to recolor my hair it really didn't help that I couldn't rinse it out because my shower was producing nothing but hot water again. Japanese utilities are a source of constant bewilderment. Take the shower, for example: when I first turn it on, all I get is cold water, which is normal, right? But after a bit, it becomes hot enough to cook lobsters, a shooting waterfall of pain. That's a tad difficult to bathe in. How it's possible for the shower to consistently produce only boiling liquid despite the fact I've turned off the hot water tap is a mystery one can only hope to solve quickly while watching one's hair turn purple.

Similarly, my microwave has become a useless box, since I managed to fuck it up so badly by randomly pushing buttons written in *kanji* that it now refuses to heat anything. The fridge makes everything room temperature no matter which way I turn the little knob. Why my Japanese class thought it would be a good idea for me to learn the kanjis for cat, bird, dog, and horse, but not for any controls on the freaking microwave, stove, or refrigerator, I've no idea. The only mixed blessing is the air conditioner, which takes the temperature steadily down to about minus forty. I have to sleep with a hat and gloves just to survive the night, but on the plus side I can leave the fridge door open and keep all the hard-boiled eggs and half-eaten cans of mackerel frosty cold.

Yet despite an arctic room, useless microwave, refrigerator, and purple hair, I remain strangely optimistic about living in Japan. The fall weather is gradually starting to arrive, and no doubt the change of seasons will bring good things. I can't wait to find out how the heater works.

Working for an Eikaiwa—What's not to Like?

The Land of the Rising Sun isn't for everyone. But like Sirens to sailors, Japan exerts a pull on the unwary to the point that any job, no matter how miserable, seems tolerable in exchange for a brief encounter. I was among that number. In retrospect, I should've lashed myself to the mast.

Now, you can't put the words "Japan, "miserable," and "job" into a sentence without mentioning "*eikaiwa*," in the next. Try it—physically impossible. Jobs at *eikaiwa* (English conversation schools) are plentiful, due to the ample supply of Japanese folks willing to pay to learn English. And, perhaps fortunately for you, the teaching qualifications are close to nonexistent. If you speak English and have a college degree, Congratulations, you're qualified. A number of eikaiwa schools will even arrange an apartment and help sort through official hassles like a visa, health insurance, bank account, and taxes. Plus, the salary's reasonably good. Yo, what's not to like?

To understand why working for an eikaiwa will be your personal hell on earth, let's begin by looking at a typical job ad:

Work 40 hours per week, teaching 25 class hours per week. Tue-Fri 1-10pm, and Sat 10am-7pm. Salary of 220,000 yen per month.

Actually, that sounds pretty good. 220,000 yen is about $2,000 U.S. a month. Not bad if you're a new graduate whose last job was The Foot Locker. 40 hours a week? Well, you'd do that anywhere, and you're really only "working" 25 of the hours, which is less than a part-time job. It's like a paid vacation to live in the land of your dreams. Sign me up.

So I dropped by the supermarket last week. It was around midnight and I thought I'd just pick up a couple of cocktails on my way home. Then, as I passed through the refrigerated section, I saw a package of sushi for 70% off. Cheap raw fish— how could that not be a good thing? I'll spare you the details from several hours curled up in a ball, but let's just say sometimes when things looks too good to be true, they are.

But back to the eikaiwa. If 25 hours of teaching per week sounds like 25 classes, or five a day, you're well on your way to buying a package of expired tuna rolls. You're teaching by the hour, not the class. So if classes are 50 minutes long, you'll teach 30 classes a week, or 6 a day. Even still, you'll have ten minutes between each class, during which time you can relax. Just kidding. You don't get a break. You have to talk with students. A teacher talking to students? Sounds a whole lot like teaching. So in reality, you're doing 5 extra 10-minute mini-classes every day. That brings your teaching load up to about seven hours a day, during which time you'll be lucky to take a whiz or gulp down some cold coffee.

Now, reality check time. Teaching looks easy. Kind of how being President of the U.S. looks easy. But it's an incredibly tough job, both mentally and physically. Teaching, that is. Being President is, by comparison, a piece of cake. As an eikaiwa teacher, you're on your feet all day long, talking, writing, gesturing, with people watching every time you want to scratch your privates. Four hours of teaching feels like 8 hours doing any normal job. Hope you don't get itchy. You're an actor putting on a one-person show, on stage seven hours, every day. Then picture the audience not laughing at any of your jokes because you're speaking a language they don't understand.

I speak from experience with a lot of hard jobs. As a construction worker, I shoveled, carried, and hammered things from sunup to sundown. As a programmer, I stared into a computer screen 12 hours a day. Night shift at a convenience store? Did it. Bike messenger? Yup. Corporate manager? Uh huh. Foot Locker? Yeah. Dishwasher at a Chinese restaurant? Jeez, did that too. And in Japan, I've done a dozen more jobs. The conclusion? Did you know that when Sinead O'Connor sang *Nothing Compares to You*, she was singing about an eikaiwa? Little known fact.

But it gets worse. The typical contract that states you'll be teaching "25 class-hours per week" also includes a clause for overtime. This means the school can require you to teach additional classes in exchange for overtime pay. Now, I like money as much as the next guy, but I also wouldn't hit myself in the head with a brick for a few extra yen. After six hours of teaching, interspersed with 10-minute bursts of talking to students, I'd choose a cinder block over more hours of teaching. But since I had no choice, I watched my workload shoot up over 35 classes a week, plus the additional 10 minutes between each class. I wasn't the only one, of course, as all the other teachers were in the same boat. The first time a teacher passed out in class and got carried to the hospital, I was like, What the hell's going on? The second time it happened I was like, Oh, that again. The third teacher that went down, I just stepped over her lifeless body and walked into class. No time for the dead and dying—gotta teach English.

A lot of people complain about other aspects of eikaiwa work, like having to take out the trash, vacuum the carpets, sell study materials, or get chewed out by the manager. But honestly, those are just minor annoyances. The real problem is in the fundamental structure of the contract, and the godless desire of the company to work you to death. Oh, and a schedule that gives you only Sundays and Mondays off. Good luck getting together with anybody outside of the eikaiwa world. Let's meet for beer—how's Monday afternoon for you? But on the plus side, you do get to live and work in Japan, at least until something better comes along. Like moving to America.

Japanese Winter, Mighty Frosty

It's been a bitterly cold winter, but spring is coming. I haven't yet burned my apartment building to the ground. You gotta cherish the simple things in life.

I recently bought a space heater to save some yen on my electric bill. Before moving to Japan, I somehow pictured living in a high-rise with a panoramic city view. Champagne and lobster, that kind of thing. The dream did not include sitting on the floor of a dark, four-story building, staring at the factory across the street while wearing a beanie and drinking cans of *chu-hi* in front of a tiny heater. Reality can be so cruel.

Fortunately, to help me survive the harsh climate, the Tokyo Electric Company sent a special pamphlet with cartoons of a girl and her cat staying blissfully warm by following simple steps. The language was perplexing, but from the pictures I gathered that if the cat simply kept the toilet lid closed, everything would be toasty. I was quite pleased to learn this, and immediately went and put down the lid. Then I waited. I also considered getting a cat, but I thought I'd first see how well the toilet bit worked. Disappointingly, the apartment didn't exactly become tropical like I'd hoped. It just made it one step harder to pee.

A more helpful suggestion from the pamphlet was to close my curtains. Unlike the toilet lid, this did eventually make the place warmer. Unfortunately, during the day it also forced me to choose between heat and sunlight, but so long as I kept my apartment dark as a cave and huddled around my heater, things were just grand.

The one mistake I made this season was washing my sheets and cleaning the place up. Initially, I felt good about it, but housework always makes me hungry. This feeling was exacerbated by the sudden odor of delicious popcorn, which was odd, considering I wasn't cooking anything. There was also something peculiar happening to my futon cover, which appeared to be on fire. But of course this was only because while changing the sheets I'd thrown it on top of the heater and it was, actually, on fire.

Around this time, I realized my bedding had become a roaring inferno in the middle of my otherwise tidy apartment, right next to the closed curtains. I never really thought of the ceiling as low, but then I'd never lit a fire under it either. On the plus side, the room was finally nice and warm. I rapidly looked left, then right, but no amount of looking either direction or saying oh-jeezus-oh-man seemed to make the flames any smaller, so eventually I grabbed an un-fiery futon edge and dragged it through the kitchen into the shower. You'd be surprised how much smoke one futon cover can produce.

Even in Japan, there is a God, as evidenced by the fact that the smoke alarm did not go off. I could just picture explaining in Japanese why this was "no big deal" to the crusty evil lady next door while she whacked me about the head with an umbrella. I now know the reason Japanese God gave me a second chance: because He doesn't want me to do housework. Far be it from me to challenge divine intervention. Lord, I now await your instructions never to wash the dishes again.

One Really Long Year in Japan

Fellow citizens, our long national nightmare is finally over. Let us now embark upon that shining road to recovery. Of course, by "national" I mean Japan, and "long nightmare" as in my teaching English here while everyone else listens to my bitching about it. In retrospect, I guess I should've read my one-year school contract more carefully. I assumed "one agrees to be poked by devils while drowning in a pool of anguish" was just boilerplate contractual stuff. Who knew they meant it literally?

When I arrived, I had simple career goals. Specifically, bailing on my *eikaiwa* job and befriending the *yakuza*, using a mix of rough but charming Japanese. They would encourage me to sell knock-off Rolexes, get a full-back tattoo, shake down some ramen shop owners, and engage in crazy money laundering schemes. I thought the latter had a particularly nice ring to it. It's like you're taking money—which is already great stuff—and you're making it cleaner. How could that not be a good thing?

Shockingly though, the whole yakuza gig never materialized. Despite being repeatedly solicited by Shinjuku doormen with rock-star hair and pointy shoes, none of the offers I received resembled an employment opportunity. To my dismay, I had to resort to doing what my school had brought me here for—namely, teaching classes. Oh, the horror.

It's not that teaching English isn't fun. Sure, riding an elevator is kind of fun, too. You just wouldn't want to do it all day, every day. Teaching, like fried food, is great in limited quantities, but too much leaves you tired and disgusted with yourself. Late at night, while I wasn't at work, or inventing metaphors about work, I lay on my apartment floor, watching YouTube videos of the U.S. Army Rangers' training program. There was something comforting and familiar about watching military guys crawling through the jungle. Check it out—every day, surviving on two or three hours of sleep, then getting up and sprinting through the rain, standing at attention for hours, and having to do complex mental tasks while being yelled at and humiliated by superiors. Well, that's teaching English for you. But being an Army Ranger seems pretty hard too.

Where I'll go from here, no one knows. From my boss, I got a handshake, an envelope of cash, and the Japanese equivalent of "don't let the door hit your ass on the way out." Friends say they're worried about my lack of future planning. To which I can only answer, since when is lying in bed watching TV with a giant plastic bottle of *shochu* not a plan? But, people, let us be unburdened. I shall go back to being the man of leisure I was born to be, while you can resume doing whatever you did before you had to listen to me bitch and moan about work all the time. Free at last, free at last. Thank God Almighty, we're free at last.

Back on the Chrome Horse

Thanks to the Swine Flu, I was able to buy my first Japanese bicycle. If that Pig Influenza hadn't sidelined me in bed for a week, I'd have surely blown another paycheck on yet one more all-you-can-drink karaoke session. But as it happened, once my fever broke, my wallet contained a spare hundred bucks worth of yen, so off I went to the bike store. I bought the largest bike I could find. It was still tiny, like riding a midget, but also just as fun.

A bike's a great way to get around. I went to the next town. Wow, just like my town. From there I found a lazy, tree-lined downhill. I was like, Man, cycling is so relaxing. Gradually, the downhill got a bit steeper, I stopped pedaling, the trees ended, and then without warning my meandering path turned into a highway entrance. I was like, Ah jeez, not cool. Suddenly there was this terrible truck roaring behind me and a tall railing keeping me from the sidewalk. Faster and faster went the tiny bicycle until the handlebars started shaking and I felt a sudden need to urinate. Something flew off one of the wheels and cracked on the concrete. Well, probably didn't need whatever that was anyway. At this point the truck decided it would be a good idea to start honking. So there's a giant white guy on a teenie-weenie bike entering the freeway at a hundred miles an hour, and you think honking will improve matters? Thanks for the support.

A bike's a great way to get mind-bendingly lost. Once the road leveled out, the truck blew past, and I tossed bike and self over the shaky railing, I was far, far from home. Like in Kansas far. No way was I going back up that hill, so I thought, The hell, I'll just loop around. I figured if I only made left-hand turns, I'd soon circle back home. I'm smart like that. I made three perfect left turns before coming to a halt in an alley, where a glaring old man said, in English, "No way." So helpful, the Japanese.

There are lots of maps on signboards in Japan, but for some

reason they're all in Japanese. And as I rode around triangulating my position based upon the sun, wind direction, and Tokyo Tower, I kept bumping into things, notably other bikes and people. Now, as far as I can tell, there are no rules whatsoever about riding a two-wheeler in this country. Right side of the road, left side of the road, sidewalk, shopping arcade, it makes no difference. I succeeded in pissing off guys in suits and knocking over grannies like bowling pins.

Eventually, by using my wrist watch as a sextant and asking directions in slobbering Japanese, I found Denny's, which wasn't home but still was nothing short of awesome, since I had a craving for a massive breakfast, famished as I was from all that riding. Denny's also has a really nice automated bike parking system, at least until you use it. I rolled my front wheel up a thin ramp and suddenly jaws locked around it. Then I couldn't get the bloody thing out. Some crazy Japanese device had taken control of my midget bike. So I had breakfast anyway, then came back out and cried in front of the bike vending machine until some schoolgirl showed me how to pay for my bike's release. Two bucks to park a bike? It's going to be a while before I eat at Denny's again.

I'm pretty sure the cops in Japan have nothing better to do than to give me directions, which is a good thing since I asked at every police box until I finally found my way back to my village, took a long bath, and resolved never to leave the house again. It's a big, confusing country out there. Probably best to just stay home.

The Great Tohoku Earthquake

When the Tohoku earthquake happened, I was sitting at my tiny Japanese desk, in the middle of a giant Japanese office, in the middle of Tokyo, just hating life. I was working elbow to elbow with about a hundred people, facing a row of unsmiling coworkers across from me, crouched in front of my PC, without speaking from morning till night. The most exciting part of the day was lunchtime, when we'd all take out our *bento* boxes and consume nutrition in silence. I couldn't imagine it could get any worse.

Funny about that. You never really think about something like the floor too much, until it starts jumping around, which is what suddenly began happening. In an instant, our building went from a solid structure to a loose bunch of concrete and glass rocking side to side, as a hundred people gave out a collective, cautious "Whoooaaa."

Now, in preparation for just such an emergency, our company had provided every employee with a liter of water and two cans of bread. I'd long ago gotten used to strange foods in Japan, so the idea of bread in a can didn't seem particularly abnormal. What I really couldn't figure out though was why we hadn't also been provided with, say, a can of tuna and a jar of mayo. But in any case, I reached for those cans, since that seemed to be the only thing within my control. But bread or no bread, it soon became apparent the shaking had moved from the floor to the walls and ceiling. You could see the windows starting to flex. We all looked at each other for about a second as a deep rumbling came up through the building, and then, with a tremendous crash, all hell broke loose.

I learned I don't really fit beneath my Japanese-sized desk. It was kind of like a cat trying to crawl into a paper bag, where he gets his little head in but the rest of his big body is sticking out. The floor started going up and down and things came off the walls and people started to yell and scream. I opened my cans of bread and prayed, but it seemed like the walls wouldn't stop shaking no matter how much bread I ate, which by the way tastes terrible. By the time it was over I'd polished off both cans and was halfway through my bottle of emergency water. There were crumbs everywhere.

It was only later that the severity of things became apparent, as news of the tsunami started coming in. I don't think anybody realized how bad it was at first, but as we listened to the radio and watched the TV, it started to look heavy. Like really heavy. And then, because we're in Japan and the Japanese have about one response to everything, we went quietly back to work. A huge aftershock happened a few minutes later, but since I was all out of rations, I just kept on working and shaking along with everyone else.

When evening came, it seemed there was another problem, as the trains had stopped, meaning no one could go home. My coworkers just kept on working throughout the night, until they fell asleep at their desks. I left the office, and my first thought was, as always, to crash in the corner of some bar. But every izakaya and noodle shop I went to was either packed or closed, so that idea was out. So I had a few convenience store cocktails to sharpen my crisis management skills, and then started walking home. The sidewalks were teeming with people in dark suits trudging forward, and the overpasses so crowded that we waited in line just to climb the steps. Taxis, cars, nothing could move. At one point, I boarded a bus, but the traffic was so heavy that it only went forward about a yard in twenty minutes, so I got off again and kept on walking.

It got pretty cold. There were no hats or gloves left in the stores, so I bought a surgical mask, which helped keep my face warmer, and cans of hot coffee for each pocket. I walked. I looked at maps. I asked directions. And I walked some more. I hoped I would find a running shoe store or maybe steal a bike, but neither happened, so I kept going in my pointy Japanese shoes. I walked for five hours before I made it to Ikebukuro, went straight to a bar, had some corn nuts and beer, and rested. Then I walked some more. Maybe another two hours.

When I got home, my old wooden house was still standing, although some tiles had fallen off the roof, one of the beams had split, and my room was an utter mess. Clothes and books were scattered everywhere. Then I remembered it always looks that way, so I couldn't really blame the earthquake.

Today, it's lovely and warm, and sakura blossoms are drifting in the wind. But even now, the aftershocks continue. Maybe we've had a hundred or more. The reports of the death toll up north and the nuclear meltdown have become real. The stores are empty of food and tonight, again, the lights will be out all over Tokyo. Why does Japan have to be so beautiful and yet so terrifying?

I Am a Japanese Farmer

Did you know that when you get a coffee from a convenience store in Japan, it comes in a can, not a styrofoam cup? For real, it does. My favorite brand is Black Boss, just because it sounds hilarious. For some odd reason, Tommy Lee Jones is the company spokes-model. They have his old, wrinkly-ass face on posters all over the nation, above the headline "Black Boss." Personally, I think Rick Ross would've been a better choice. Is that racist? Yeah, probably. But I still think so.

In other news, last weekend I worked on a farm. While I thought it would be kind of exhilarating in a back-to-nature sort of way, it was more like hitting stalks of wheat with a bamboo stick for eight hours. Man, working on a farm sucks. Being a farmer must really suck. All I did what hit this effing wheat with a stick and little wheatlets would fall off. Like you ever hear the expression–separating the wheat from the chaff? Well, me neither, but that's apparently what I did. And it was kinda cool, to see where flour actually comes from, for about a second. And then I was like, Man, I need a break. Figured I'd drink me a Black Boss and get my relax on. But this old farmer guy gave me the stink eye and told me to keep whacking, so I had to do that shit till noon, all covered in wheat dust.

The stuff gets all up in your nose and eyes. It's like working in a sand factory. It seems we were involved in an early stage of soba noodle production, but all I know is I never saw noodle one. I was like, you mean this is where food comes from? How is that even possible? Nature is so fascinating.

Later we planted onions and harvested *sato imo*, which are small, tasteless, slimy potatoes. I said, you know, there's probably a reason McDonald's doesn't sell five billion supersized *sato imo* every year, d'ya think? But nobody did and everybody just kept hoeing dirt like mad, so I shut up and hoed. Later, we picked shitake mushrooms off of logs.

"How you know they're not poisonous?" I asked.

"If you wake up the next morning..." said Stink Eye guy.

I waited for him to complete the sentence, but apparently that was it.

That night I slept in a farmhouse with these two old snoring Japanese dudes on a tatami floor and tossed and turned while praying to Japanese God I wouldn't die of mushroom poisoning. But fortunately the mess of beer and boiled crabs we had for dinner acted as a powerful antidote, so I just woke up with a hangover and then whacked more wheat with a stick and only wished I was dead. At the end of the second day I got a bag of rice and four hundred tangerines for my efforts. Seriously, what the hell's a single guy gonna do with four hundred tangerines? My skin's already turning orange from trying to eat them all. Those damn things sure are juicy though.

New Year's in Japan

I hate the cold, so don't ask me why I went to the snowiest possible place for New Year's. Japanese New Year's is like Christmas in the U.S., only without all the presents and with better food. So I went to Hokkaido, where there was a ton of snow and we mostly stayed inside and drank beer. Once that ran out, we drank wine. On New Year's Eve, we ate long soba noodles to ensure longevity, and the next morning sticky *mochi* rice in soup, which is about the best way to guarantee a short life. That stuff's like eating white Playdough. Two weeks ago my girlfriend's uncle died when a clump of *mochi* stuck in his throat and he couldn't breathe. This happens every year in Japan, but people keep eating the stuff. Gotta love tradition.

Highlights of the trip, other than freezing my ass off, included going to the Sapporo Brewery for *sukiyaki* and beer. My gal was like, Look at all the *illumination*. That's what they call Christmas lights in Japan. We stood outside in the snow and it was about minus a hundred. I looked. Very sparkly. Let's go see if there's illumination in the tasting room, I suggested. But no, we had to see the illumination from different *angles*. You know, all those giant windows, I noted, the folks at this brewery installed those for the express purpose of seeing the exact same lights from inside a nice warm room while drinking beer like a civilized person and not some freaking polar bear. Ah whoops, shouldn't have said that, because that made her pouty and then she wanted to go back in, and I ended up saying no, no, let's see it from just one more frozen angle. Jeez, women.

On the last day, we went skiing and it was refreshing to get some exercise. I'm such an excellent skier. Sorry, meant to use the past tense. I'll edit that later. Like, Ken Seeroi grew up skiing, but it'd kinda been a few years.

Japanese mountains are strangely a lot steeper than they appear, and they look pretty steep. At one point I went over a small mogul, got a bit sideways, but managed to stick the landing. I was like, yeah Seeroi, you still got it. And as I'm racing down the slope, I notice there's somebody's ski alongside me. Like some fool had lost a ski, just like my ski. And then my left boot suddenly seemed kind of lonely in the breeze and I thought, yeeaah, maybe gonna need that ski at some point. Japanese snow's not as soft as you'd think, is what I've learned.

After not dying on the ski slope, we came home and had beer—also quite refreshing—along with sushi, sake, and boiled shrimp. Then somebody passed out on the floor and missed the remainder of New Year's Day. So basically, I can't remember much of Sapporo, but I'm told I had a great nap. I got back yesterday, and was greeted by a small earthquake. Or maybe I'm still drunk, I don't know.

It's been several months since that terrifying Tohoku quake, and now the aftershocks have mostly subsided, which is fine by me. Actually, since I now live out in the rice paddies, even if we had one it'd probably just knock over a barn or something. At Christmas time, I taught the local farm kids about Santa Claus, but all they wanted to know was what happens when flying reindeer take a dump. So I told them Yeah, it's just like when birds poo. If it hits you it's good luck. Jeez, Japanese kids.

Living in the Palace. Leopalace

"My next-door neighbor smokes on the balcony," I said. "Wonder if I should say something to him?"

"I wouldn't," replied Suwako, "he might knife you."

Suwako and I were having dinner, balancing half a dozen plates and bowls on a table the size of a checkerboard, and I was like, How's that your first thought? Japan's supposedly this great, safe country, and your immediate reaction is, Yeah, he'll probably shank you? That's not very neighborly.

So I never said anything about the annoying smoke and instead just ran the fan on high beside the balcony door, which I'm sure he could hear. We're very passive-aggressive like that in Japan.

This was my Leopalace apartment. Gotta love the name— it's like you're a lion, living in a palace. Leo palace. Assuming your palace has the dimensions of a walk-in closet and your closet's the size of a suitcase.

Now if you live in Japan, you've probably already wound up in said Palace, and not just because it's a nationwide chain that offers low-budget accommodations appropriate for midgets. Sorry, little people. It's that they'll rent to anybody. And seriously freaking anybody, including midgets. Naturally, this comes with some pros and cons.

So the first week I lived in the Palace, somebody left a condom on the landing leading up to the second floor. That didn't seem too palatial, so I'm entering "condom" into the negative column. How it got there and whether it was used or not, I wasn't trying to know, but the fucking thing lay there for two days like an old sock. Now, there's only one staircase for the whole building so you know everybody's just stepping over it. Jeezus. Finally, I just picked it up with a plastic bag and threw it in the trash. Why is Ken Seeroi the only person in this damn nation who takes any action? That's a rhetorical question.

Which speaks to the real drawback of Leopalace

apartments—all those damn *foreigners*. My building was a motley collection of Chinese, Nepalese, and Indonesians, living two or more to a room, plus a few Japanese folks, and me, Token McWhitey. Now, I've got nothing against people of other nations, but—and trying not to sound racist here—they're just not *like* us. And by "us," I mean of course me and the other Japanese people.

Okay, so let's talk trash, the national obsession. Every Japanese person knows you gotta throw out the burnable stuff in a special "burnable garbage" bag. Non-burnable goes into the "non-burnable" bag. You get the idea. And every type of trash is assigned its own personal day of the week for pick-up. Sure, kind of a pain in the ass, but hey, welcome to the nation.

So every week, the Japanese folks and I would dutifully wait until Tuesday morning before carrying down our burnable trash. But the fucking Chinese, Nepalese, and Indonesian folks—and remember, trying not to sound racist here—would just dump any and all garbage whenever they felt like it into a big pile in front of the building, without using the specially designated bags. When this shit starts to bother you, you really know you've been in Japan too long.

Now, on the plus side, I actually loved my apartment. Sure, it was half the size of a Motel 6 room, but it was right in the middle of the city, near shopping, a couple cool parks, and most importantly, a fantastic row of bars, which helped greatly in coping with the tobacco and trash.

It also came equipped with a washer, a/c, microwave, internet, and well-endowed young lady from Hong Kong named Crystal. I thought the latter a particularly nice perk, although I saw no immediate need to mention that to Suwako.

In an interesting design twist, despite the miniscule floor plan, each apartment had a loft. I used mine for storage, but Crystal had put her futon up there, so in the evenings we'd climb the shaky aluminum ladder to make out, sleep, and most of all escape the fleas. Technically, you weren't allowed any pets, but then you weren't supposed to throw out burnable trash on Wednesdays either, so fuck it, in for a pound and all, Crystal had adopted a cute stray cat named Mr. Butts.

And Mr. Butts' butt was full of fleas. No amount of brushing the little bastard seemed to reduce the infestation, although the vermin apparently had a devil of a time climbing the ladder. As did I after the six pack and bottle of red wine Crystal and I routinely polished off. Still, it was comfortable enough once you were up there, kind of like a low tent.

And then I woke up and had to pee. Now, another feature of the Palace is that it comes with blackout curtains, which keep the place super dark. And somehow those, combined with the beer, wine, an incredible urge to urinate, and the fact I believed I was in a tent and not nine feet off the ground contributed to my missing a rung and pitching off into the darkness, reflexively peeing all the way down.

So that was a little painful and a tad embarrassing, but fortunately the Seeroi's are a long line of shameless and sturdy people with exceptionally flexible bones. So I just lay on the damp carpet, snuggled up to Mr. Butts, and slept till morning, when I woke up covered in fleas. Still, all in all, the Palace was a pretty great place to live, although I might recommend purchasing a few flea collars, possibly wearing one yourself, and not putting your bed in the sky.

The Japanese Name Game Switcheroo

At first, you might think Japanese folks place great importance on addressing others properly. After all, it's the nation where even elephants are called *Zou-san*. That's Mr. Elephant to you.

The reality is this naming convention works flawlessly until someone who looks "foreign" enters the scene, at which point thousands of years of custom go straight out the window.

So I was at this party last Saturday, and found myself talking with two guys a little younger than myself. One fellow was tall with great hair, while the other was a bit shorter and kind of doughy. They didn't know each other, and so they introduced themselves using last names, as Japanese people do. Then they asked my name, and I said "Seeroi." "Seeroi?" said Great Hair. "What's your first name?" When I told him "Ken," he then re-introduced himself using his first name, at which point Doughboy followed suit, and for the rest of the night I was "Ken," while they still referred to each other by their last names. The entire conversation took place in Japanese, but clearly everything changes when you talk to a white guy.

Well, what about my last name? And can't a brother get a little "*san*" up in here?

Before moving to Japan, I never thought or cared about how people addressed me. Ken, Kenneth, Kenny—hey, if it makes you happy, cool. I just don't want to be singled out, especially because of my race. Look, I know I'm white; you don't need to give me a complex about it.

In Japanese, I always introduce myself in the Japanese format of last name, first name. In which case, I'm invariably called by my first name. Sometimes I'll even say only my last name, as Japanese folks do. If so, I'm certain to be asked my first name, and then referred to by it. This happens, oh, ten out of ten times.

When I taught grade school, the students would stand and bow to greet both the Japanese teacher and myself. With a loud voice they'd chant "Good morning Yamaguchi Sensei and...Ken." The lesson was clear: people who look Japanese are addressed by their last names. That's yellow privilege. For people who look "not Japanese," all bets are off. Maybe "racism" is too strong a word, but I've yet to meet the "foreigner" who's referred to by last name only.

So I've put this case to Japanese people: if they went to an English-speaking country where everyone was on a first-name basis, like Ryan, Sam, and Abby, would they want to be called Ms. Tanaka or Mr. Honda? No way. They all agree that'd make them feel weird. So could they understand why I wouldn't want to receive differential treatment in Japan? They certainly could. Yeah, we see your point. That makes complete sense, Ken. Ah, Japanese folks. You're consistent if nothing else.

When I request to be called by my last name, I'm always met with the same response. But *Ken*, we just want to be *friendly* with you! And I'm like, Why me? Your other coworkers, the acquaintances you've known for years—what about them? You want the school kids to be friendly with the English teacher, but not the History or P.E. teacher? Why do I have to be the friendly one? I am Frosty the fucking snowman. Note the color of my skin and two eyes made out of coal.

About the only recourse I can think of is to legally change my name to something more Japanese, like Sakamoto Ryouma. Chinese and Korean people do this all the time. But if I tried it, I already know what'd happen. There'd be a moment of silence, followed by a burst of laughter, and then, "Yeah right. What's your *real* name?" And after that, they'd call me Ken.

Surprising Service in Japan

I went to a small, ramshackle Japanese restaurant this evening, and the impossible happened. Namely, I ordered, ate, paid, and left. Eats, shoots, and leaves. Sorry, too obtuse? Anyhow, the food was great, as Japanese cuisine always is, but the service...well, I was in *shocku*. Which is how you'd pronounce "shocked" if you were five years old or Japanese.

Specifically, the hostess seated me and handed me a menu. A waiter came and took my order. A tray of soba, rice, tempura, and pickles appeared, and when I was finished, I paid at the register. Everyone spoke perfect Japanese and treated me like a human being. Yeah, that'll never work.

Clearly, the owner has no idea how to run a Japanese restaurant. So to prevent this from ever happening again, it might be good to look at how more experienced restauranteurs deal with the not-so-teeming-masses of foreigners (or *gaijin*, if you must) of which I'm apparently one.

First of all, when I walk in the door, the appropriate response is to freeze and stare. If any words come out of your open mouth, they should be either "Japanese OK?" or "No English menu." Now I'm glad I chose your restaurant. Please note the correct pronunciation is *"Englishu."*

Then reply to the next thing I say—regardless of what it is—by remarking on how amazing my Japanese is. Please choose from one of the following: *"jyouzu," "umai,"* or *"pera pera."* A *"sugoi"* would also be a nice touch.

At this point I'll feel like I'm blending in, so allow me a few moments to glance at the menu, but watch me closely from the corner of your eye. Can I read it? Nah, I'm just pretending. After I randomly point at something, feel free to query me about my dietary preferences. Can I drink green tea? Eat *natto*? Have I ever tried *umeboshi*? Express surprise at my answers.

Now it's time for a few personal questions. Try something original like, "Where are you from?" or "How long have you been in Japan?" Don't forget to ask how old I am and whether or not I'm married. If my food arrives, don't let that stop you. We're having a conversation.

By now we're practically old friends, so don't hesitate to invite others to talk with me, especially drunk salarymen. Takeda-san over there spent a summer in Missouri. Maybe he'd like to sit with me? Of course he would. If there's anybody within a five-mile radius who speaks English, be especially sure to introduce them. Calling your relatives on the phone and then handing it to me is also a good option. Look, I met a foreigner! Talk to him. This is what I want when I go out to eat.

If I manage to finish my meal and show any indication of hoping to leave, make sure everyone I've spoken with gives me a business card, shakes my hand, and exchanges email and phone numbers. One can never have too much email.

See, providing great service in Japan isn't that hard. With just a little effort, you can make all your "foreign visitors" feel right at home. And I'll make sure to leave you a great review on Yelp Japan.

Navigating a Japanese Starbucks

The first time I walked into a Japanese Starbucks, I thought I was ready. It's pretty easy, really. "Large" translates to "grande," in some bizarro Italian-English-Japanese word hybrid, and "coffee" is just a bastardized pronunciation of the same: "*kohee.*" Even "hot" is, well, "*hotto.*" Can you really just turn any English word into Japanese by adding a vowel to the end? *Starbucksu.* Yeah, apparently so. Just like Spanish.

And really, how complicated could the process be? Coffee's about all they sell, so they'll definitely figure it out. At least that's what I thought.

It was a Starbucks in Ginza, Tokyo. I remember it clearly because it was a sunny day and I was sweating like a Shiba dog, having just walked back from a sushi lunch in Tsukiji wearing a suit. The moment I stepped through the door, a young lady in black and green greeted me. I was ready. "*Hotto kohe...*" I started to say.

But instead of saying "Welcome," she blurted out, "Right now, all the seats are full," in Japanese. I understood the words all right, but why was she saying them? I looked behind me, like maybe she was talking to someone else, but it was like the Sahara back there. Still, once I make a plan, I stick with it.

"One *hotto grande kohee,*" I said in Japanese, plus a couple other languages.

"Sorry," she replied, "all our seats are full."

"Hmm. That's all well and good," I continued, "but I'd still like a cup of *hotto* coffee."

"Is it okay that the seats are full?" she asked.

"Hey lady, fine by me." I said. "You gotta make a profit, so keep doin' what you're doin'. By the way, do you think I could possibly get a cup of coffee up in here? You do sell it, right?" I could feel that familiar perplexed feeling starting to creep in.

But she'd obviously also made a plan she was sticking to, so she continued, "I'm sorry, but even the second floor is full."

"Hmm," I said, "perhaps you've mistaken me for your

architect, but I don't see how that's relevant to Ken getting a cup of coffee."

"So you would like a hot grande coffee?" she asked.

"To receive one would be marvelous."

"You do understand that our seats are full," she said. And around we went.

Okay, let's zoom out. First of all, I'm no novice to Starbucks, having invested the monetary equivalent of a college education there, one steaming mug at a time. Damn your addictive dark-roasted beans. And in the U.S., when you walk into the place, you order a cup of coffee and that's what you get, at least after the employee finishes updating her Facebook page on her iPad. Where you sit—hey, that's your problem. Make friends with someone at a table, take your coffee outside, stand by the garbage cans—it's entirely up to you.

But in Japan, the thinking is different. Before they serve you, they want to be sure you aren't confounded by the lack of chairs. Japanese folks aren't real good with contingencies. If it's packed, they may line you up to wait for a seat, unlike in the U.S. where you circle the room and snatch up the first available spot in an adult version of Musical Chairs. I recommend open-carrying firearms, as this increases your chances somewhat. Greatest country on earth, clearly.

This type of procedural misunderstanding doesn't end at Starbucks, of course, and it's one challenging aspect of coming to Japan. Language ability only gets you so far. Knowing the established pattern of every transaction is equally important. Which is to say that even if you know zero Japanese, you can easily handle interactions simply by knowing what to expect.

For example, when I went to buy a pack of gum at 7-Eleven, the cashier was like, "Seal okay?" I froze. Seal okay? What could it possibly mean? After years of studying Japanese, I couldn't begin to parse the question. Of course, no Japanese person would ever help you out by using actual words, like

"Would you like a plastic bag or can I just affix this tape sticker as proof of purchase?" On the other hand, I quickly learned words were unnecessary, because if I just stood there like a chimp, they'd slap a seal on the gum anyway. So that saved me one whole word, which you never know when you might need.

Similarly, when you go to the supermarket, the cashier's likely to ask if you've brought your own bag. If you answer "yes" (my default answer to every question I don't understand), you'll be stuck having to carry your groceries home in your hands. As much as that sucks, going back and asking for a bag would be to admit not having understood Japanese perfectly, which is clearly out of the question. This is how I discovered I can fit two beers into the back pockets of my jeans and a large fish sausage in the front. And now I'm happy to see you.

I went against my own default answer the first time I bought a bottle of *sake* in the basement of a Japanese department store. The clerk asked, "Is this for home consumption?" and I was like, Hmm, if I say "yes," he'll know I'm a drunk, so how about we go with "no"? At which point he proceeded to wrap it like a Christmas present. I can't see why anybody'd want that. Sure, it looks nice, but all those ribbons, plastic, and foil just get between you and the booze.

At restaurants, dry cleaners, gas stations, there are dozens of these types of patterns in Japan. Well, maybe every country has them, I don't know. The bottom line is, no matter how amazing your Japanese is, it won't help a bit until you've mastered the flow of things. And even then, eh, probably not. You're better off communicating the way native Japanese do, with subtle gestures, grunts, and tilting your head a lot. Soon, people will be all, "Oh, your Japanese is so good." And you'll be like, "Unngh." Yep, now that sounds a lot more natural.

How to Bow Like a Japanese

What could be more typically Japanese than bowing? Every book about Japan has something to say on the subject, so it seems important. I see a lot of visitors coming to Japan and bowing like crazy, so perhaps they've all read the same book.

It's common knowledge, if not entirely correct, that bowing's a sign of respect, gratitude, or apology in Japanese society. And there's no shortage of information on how to do it properly, how deeply one should bow, or what to do with your hands. There's just one missing piece...

So I was in a bar last week. Big surprise, I know. And by the end of the night, as is the custom of my people, I'd made friends with about fifty salarymen. What can I say? I'm like sugar to them. Then, seeing as I'd had a rather plentiful number of cocktails and had to wake up the next day before noon (something I try to avoid), I decided to politely make my exit. And what happened next? They all got up and started bowing. Nah, just kidding. They all started shaking my hand, of course, and sometimes both hands at once. I am everybody's favorite Raggedy Ann doll.

You know, when a Japanese guy leaves a bar, everybody doesn't rush up and start madly shaking his hand. And in America, well, basically the same thing. We just say goodbye and peace out. The last time I was back in the States, it seemed like men and women had given up shaking hands in favor of hugging. But maybe that's just San Francisco. Californians, jeez. Anyway, while America may still be the land of hamburgers and handshakes, people don't go around doling them out all willy-nilly either.

However, in the mind of a Japanese salaryman who has just polished off a bottle of *shochu*, shaking hands is what "foreigners" do. Just like how foreigners think bowing is something Japanese do.

Okay, here's three questions for you. Let's see how good your Japanese is.

1. It's 10 a.m. and you're out for a walk. On the other side of the street, you see your neighbor coming towards you. What do you say?

2. Your walk into a store at noon and the store clerk bows and greets you with "*irrashaimasei*." What do you say?

3. It's 10 p.m. and you buy two large cans of malt liquor and a bag of those fabulous Calbee black pepper potato chips. (Note: this is a purely hypothetical situation.) After you pay at the register, the clerk bows and thanks you with an "*arigatou gozaimasu*." What do you say?

If you answered, "good morning," "hello," and "you're welcome"—congratulations, you're a foreigner all right. But if you answered, "jack shit," then you've either lived in Japan for a while, or you're actually Japanese. In other words, Japanese people rarely reply to such pleasantries. Not the friendliest country actually, Japan.

So here's the missing piece: Japan has a culture based upon hierarchy. It's a Power culture. Store clerks thank you. You don't thank them. At the restaurant, you yell your order to the waitress and she comes running. She's all politeness, smiles, bowing, and deference, because that's her job. You, as a customer, have a different role, and it does not include thanking, bowing, or even acknowledging her presence. Then, when that waitress is a customer somewhere else, she'll bark her order at someone else who comes running, and hardly mumble a word of thanks. In any situation, the people on the bottom of the power equation bow and thank those above them. The people at the top don't respond in kind, and frequently don't respond at all.

Bear in mind that bowing isn't necessarily related to a person's status in society, age, or gender. It's about their role in a given situation. Who's the boss and who's the employee, who's holding the leash and who's the dog. The person who bows in one situation doesn't bow in another, and nobody bows all the time. Except old people. And they're just grateful somebody noticed they're still alive.

Japan has the reputation of being a polite nation. That's because, for tourists, everywhere they look, Japanese folks are welcoming, thanking, and bowing to them. What wonderful, simple people! They're so cute. In reality, it's about business. It's not that Japanese people are more or less polite than anyone else. It's that they're serious employees. It's their job to treat you well, in the same way that when I call MasterCard, they say "Thank you for calling." Maybe the person on the other end of the line isn't actually grateful that I called to complain about my interest rate. But then you never know. Those folks in Bangladesh are awfully polite.

So take a step back. Next time you go to a store, restaurant, or bar in Japan, don't watch the clerks and waiters. Watch the Japanese customers. Quite often, they're a whole lot less than polite. They either boss the staff around, or ignore them entirely. They certainly don't bow to the staff.

Now, you can act however you like in Japan. Bow to the mailman if that's your thing. Thanks for bringing my electric bill, dude! Hey, it's a free country. But if you've gone to the trouble of learning some Japanese and trying to understand the culture, then you might want to pay attention to what everybody else does, and try to behave similarly. Just a thought.

This isn't to say that there aren't plenty of opportunities to bow. You should absolutely show respect and appreciation towards people with whom you have a personal connection. But again, keep in mind who's thanking whom. If, for example, you give someone a gift, they should bow a bit and thank you. Or maybe they won't. Either way, as the gift-giver, you probably shouldn't be bowing to them, unless you're thanking them for something they've done. Okay, so it's a little complicated. Just keep your roles straight, is all I'm saying.

As a final note, there is, of course, the reciprocal bowing phenomenon where everyone stands around bowing like mad to everyone else in what looks like a mini aerobics class. You see this a lot after office drinking parties, where employees

past, and less time thinking about the future. We just ate our canned fish on toast and talked to the Japanese office ladies next to us. And every time we yelled out an order, the staff came running. God, it's a good country to be a customer in.

How to be Popular in Japan

I'm the most popular guy in town. And given that about a million people live in my little village, I feel that's quite a distinction. So recently, I bought a jump rope. Look, it's not easy keeping in shape in Japan. Like I'd just gotten home last Thursday night when I got a call from this old guy I teach English to. He's about seventy years old and some president of a company or something. Actually, I don't even know his name. I just call him President-san.

So I pick up the phone and he says, "Can you sing The Beatles?" And I'm like, "Who *is* this?" And he says his name, but of course I still don't know who he is because I don't know his name, and he says, "There's a band at the *izakaya*. Come here now and sing English songs!" And he says all this in Japanese, which is kind of ironic, and a bit depressing since it's my fault his English isn't getting any better. But I still hopped on my bike and reluctantly raced down there. I discovered singing with a band is a whole lot harder than karaoke. You never think about how many words are in a song until there aren't any lyrics in front of you. Still the crowd went wild when I sang "Imagine." I sound just like John Lennon.

Then on Saturday, I purchased this jump rope. It only cost a dollar, which is about the greatest deal ever. You know, it's not easy to maintain one's fitness when one's exercise for the week is biking to and from izakayas, And I took it to the park at dusk, just as it was starting to get dark. Actually, I think the Japanese word for "park" translates to English as "miserable patch of dirt." Somebody seriously needs to introduce the Japanese to the concept of grass. But since it's an open space and close to my apartment, that's where I went.

If there's something more physically challenging than jumping rope, I don't want to know what it is. Jumping rope for five minutes is like running a marathon, only harder and without semi-hot housewives handing you Gatorade. And at the end of five minutes of hopping up and down in the dirt I finally stopped and was going to quietly have a heart attack and die when I looked up and in the dark, all around me, were little pairs of eyes. Children's eyes. It was like some weird horror film, where all these little kids form a circle and close in on you from all directions. Instantly, I was mobbed by Japanese children. They wanted to know why I was jumping rope, and where I was from, and if they could too. So I said Go ahead, and didn't see my jump rope again for the next half hour. Bunch of little thieves, the lot of them.

After I finally retrieved my newest prized possession, I decided to stop by the 7-Eleven for some electrolyte replacement drink in the form of a malted beverage. That's when I noticed I had a problem. Something was missing from my wallet, and it wasn't just money as usual. It was my alien registration card. The little ID card that allows me to legally stay in this country. Somehow, somewhere, I managed to lose the only thing I actually need in Japan. Where it went, I've no idea. Well okay, it might've been that bar in Kitakyushu, but regardless, I'm an idiot. But I forged ahead and bought two giant cans of malt liquor, since nobody's ever carded me in this country anyway.

So the next day I had to go to City Hall, which was a pain in the ass. And they sent me to the police station, which was a bigger pain in the ass. And the cops were like, Where'd you lose it? And I was like, Man, I don't know. I went to this bar, sang with a band, jumped some rope, and bought some booze. That's all. And the one cop sits up and says, "Oh, you're that white guy who jumps rope." And I was like, What, you know me? And he's like, Yeah, my kids love you. And then I felt bad. Not because I thought ill of his kids, but because that nice man obviously believed his children weren't a bunch of thieving hooligans, when they clearly were.

So I got my police report and went back to City Hall, took a number, and had to wait for about an hour, and I was sure wishing I had something cool and refreshing to drink. City Hall is really boring. They have magazines and television, sure, but no internet. What kind of place is that? I made up my mind to stop by the 7-Eleven on my way home. So after a forever of watching Japanese TV with no sound, eventually they call my number. I go up to the desk and give the lady my police report and she's like, Oh, you're that white guy who sounds like John Lennon! And I was like, Jeezus, what the hell's up with you people? I need to get me a disguise like Clark Kent or something. So we talked for a while and she was thrilled as punch.

Then eventually I made it to 7-Eleven and picked up a can of some grapefruity booze and a package of these delicious potato stick things. My diet here has gone to hell. When I get to the counter I can see a flash of recognition in the clerk's face, but I shoot him a look, like, Don't you say it. And then just when I think I'm going to make it to the door without comment, another clerk comes running from the back and is all like, "Ken-san!" And so we talk and joke around for a bit. And instantly I'm in the middle of a circle, telling the whole store about how I lost my ID and the details of my new exercise program. Everyone's nodding their heads and then they all start saying how they'll buy jump ropes and come down to the park too. And I'm like, Oh my God no. In about one second I went from being the Man of Steel to being the new town gym teacher. I really gotta stop being so damn popular.

What Do You Think of Japan?

I used to think there were three possible answers to any question: yes, no, and whatever's not covered by yes and no. Like, when the waitress asks, Do you want another beer? That's a yes. Isn't it about time you thought about going home? That'd be a No, not until I get the beer I'm waiting for. And, Would you at least please stop bothering the other customers? That'd be a Well, if that's how you feel about it, then I'm leaving. Just as soon as I get my beer.

It's interview season in Japan. The weather's getting warmer, the *ume* buds are starting to appear, and maybe you could even see a bird. Yeah, like maybe in a zoo. And about this time every year I pick my two-sizes-too-small Japanese suit up from the floor of my closet, polish the front of my shoes, then head out with my resume.

I went to an interview last week. It was for a job teaching English, so for some reason unbeknownst to anyone, the entire interview was in Japanese.

I walked in and there was this chair in the middle of an enormous room, and a panel of six people sitting at a long, white table, all staring at me. I was like, Is this my chair? Why is it so far away from everyone? I sat in the chair.

Everything went pretty swimmingly. My version of speaking Japanese is to toss a bunch of nouns and verbs in semi-random order into a sentence and then stick a *desu* on the end. And that's what you get. It's not pretty, but everyone smiled and nodded at the appropriate times, so I guess they followed it okay. Actually, it was better than the time I had an interview in the States and looked down to discover the crotch of my old suit was riddled with moth-eaten holes. In the middle of the interview I realized I could literally see my own balls. True story. So at least that didn't happen.

They asked a lot of stupid questions. Why did you want to become a teacher? Hmm, maybe because I wanted to graduate from a diet of ramen noodles and instant coffee.

What's the difference between teaching children and adults? Uh, they're smaller? I don't know. That sounded plausible, so I made up some more shit and it sounded okay. And then they asked The Question: "What do you think of Japan?" And everyone leaned forward a little bit.

I heard a little voice in my head. It said, "Easy question, Ken! Knock it outta the park and let's go get a beer!"

I don't know why God gave me the little voice, because I apparently never listen to it. Instead, I had a Moment of Clarity. Right there in the middle of the enormous room, I realized that there were not three possible answers, but rather three *ways* of answering any question.

Way 1: Lies. I love this, because lies are super convenient. You just tell people what they want to hear. "Japan's great. Everyone's very respectful and thoughtful of others. People enjoy it when I speak Japanese and the language has helped me make many friends." Done and done. Now let's go get that beer.

Way 2: Naivete. This is the answer I would've given a decade ago. "I love Japan—everyone's so friendly. Everywhere I go, people say 'hello' and bow. They're very polite. Such kind people you have here!" Again, brilliant answer. Expect an offer letter by the end of the week.

Way 3: Thanks for the rope, I'll just be a minute while I wrap it around my neck. Any time I start answering a question with "Well...", I really should just shut up, because I know I'm on a cliff and about to dash my body onto the rocks below. In Japanese, this usually comes out as "Maa...", or possibly "Saa...," but either way, I'm screwed.

"Maa...", I said, "every positive has a corresponding negative, right?" I paused, and six people slowly nodded, transfixed. I kept going. "Things I like about Japan are also what I don't like. There's a flip-side. Seriously, what would I say about the U.S.? That it's great? U.S.A. Number One? Come on, that'd be simplistic. There's a ton of good and bad, all wrapped up together. Same here. These are big, complex countries," is what I said. Then I looked up to see if they were following me, and everyone was pale as a ghost. Every mouth in the room was hanging open, above pupils the size of saucer plates. And the little voice said, For the love of God, Ken, stop.

But I was on a roll. For some reason, the need for self-expression momentarily outweighed my aversion to sleeping in a box in the park. I continued, "For example, I love how clean the toilets are. But that seventy year-old granny who's gotta scrub the porcelain probably isn't too thrilled. Like, I wouldn't want to be her. And I love Japanese sushi. But I wouldn't wanna be that dude standing in place all day, slicing up raw fish. That would suck." Somehow it didn't sound as bad when I said it in Japanese, I thought.

I looked up again, and was like, Oh...my...God. Everyone was mortified. I thought the one lady was going to cry. Like, there was a tiny tear in the corner of her left eye. They all looked at each other, like, What should we do? And I was all, No, it's cool. Really, I don't mean I dislike Japan; it's just if someone tells you only good without the bad, they're either waxing you on, or haven't thought about it much. And I gave some more examples of good and bad, but somehow the more I said, the worse everyone looked, which I found strange. So finally, I stopped.

And then the man in the middle took a deep breath and said "Maa... Thank you for your honesty. We'll contact you within three weeks with the result. Thank you. Okay. Thank you, thank you." And I was like, Oh. So I stood up and bowed, and suddenly it seemed the door was really far away. But on the way out I thought, Well, that didn't go too bad, really. After all, I gave complete answers and even my grammar was pretty good. Plus the nice man in the middle thanked me a lot and bowed in return. Such an excellent country, and the people are awfully kind, really. I'm pretty sure I got the job.

The Shochu, the Yakuza, and the Hostess Bar

My New Year's resolution was to exercise more, but it's just not working out like that. All I could see was sawdust and screws when I opened my eyes this morning. It was 4 a.m. Man, I gotta quit getting up so early. But for some strange reason the room wasn't dark. So while I was trying to figure out who turned on the sun, I rolled over and there's my PC, upside-down on the pillow next to me. And then I realized I'm still fully dressed in a suit and tie, minus one sock. Well, at least I don't have to worry about putting on clothes all over again. So much trouble, really, getting dressed.

So I got up and it turns out my table had demolished itself in the middle of the night. Like one of the legs was snapped off and it had dumped everything onto my futon, along with screws and wood chips. Fortunately it's a Japanese table, so it's only about two inches tall. Like I don't even really know why I have the thing—I could just draw a rectangle on the floor and it'd be exactly as useful. And about then I figured out it was 4 p.m., not a.m., and I thought Man, I really need some breakfast, since I gotta be back at work in a couple hours. So I put on my sock and went to 7-Eleven.

Japan's a super convenient country. I picked up two rice balls and a can of miso soup. Actually, I should've stuck with corn soup, because the miso was awful. Ken Seeroi has an exceptionally refined palate for all things canned.

So while I was walking back home with a rice ball in each hand and miso soup in my pocket, I started trying to piece together the previous day. I had a pretty clear recollection of my "Business English" class, which involves speaking English at these five Japanese guys in suits while they try not to fall asleep. At one point I was writing a sentence on the whiteboard and the fat dude in front passed out, fell out of his chair, and landed at my feet. I was like, Next class, we're fitting you with a helmet.

Well, that was two hours of pure enjoyment for the whole

family. Once it ended I raced across town to an *izakaya*, which I believe is how you say "dive bar" in Japanese, where I teach this five year-old boy at a table in the back. It's always smoky and I come out smelling like roast chicken. His dad owns the place, but the little boy never calls him "Dad." Instead, he just calls him "The Boss." Kids are awesome. So I walk in and The Boss says hi and the kid looks at me and says "English, yuck!" and runs away. Only he says it in Japanese, which comes out as "*iyada*," and makes it sound even worse. Great.

So for the next hour I try to amuse him. Like I've got songs and games and puppets and shit, but all the little boy says is, "Can we finish now?" And I'm like, "No. Look, here's the funny dog! What does the funny dog say?" And he looks at me and says, "*iyada!*" Actually, I take back what I said. Kids are horrible, to tell you the truth.

I'm sure that was actually the longest hour of my life, and afterwards I went straight to the bar counter. I figured I'd have just one beer and call it a night. But this old retired guy with bushy eyebrows started talking to me and pretty soon he bought me a second beer, so I decided I'd stay another ten minutes. Funny how that works. He used to be a nuclear engineer, for real. The thing is, he had no interest in learning English or anything; he just wanted to hang out and drink and tell me about nuclear fission in Japanese. And since I love learning anything new as long as it's not in English, that made him pretty much the most awesome guy ever.

Then the more I drank, the more awesome he became. We really hit it off, and he kept saying, How about more beer? And I was like, Well, if you insist. And so we ate this whole live fish and a pizza and an omelet and he said, Want a glass of sake? And I'm all, Well, maybe just one. And so we had three, and ate some cold tofu and a pickled eggplant and some marinated squid parts, and he was like, You gotta try this shochu, and proceeded to pour me a glass. And I was like, Dude, you are the best! Seriously! Have I told you that? And he said, Yes, several times actually. And so we drank more shochu until this other old guy in a bright blue suit yelled to me, Want to play the *sanshin?* And I was like, Do I ever! This is pretty much my definition of the perfect evening.

The sanshin is this crazy 3-stringed Japanese banjo that no matter what you play sounds like it should be in a kung-fu movie. It's pretty easy to play something with only three strings because, well, it's only got three strings. That is, simple except if you've just downed several beers, a sake sampler, and half a bottle of shochu. Plus all the sheet music is written in obscure Japanese kanji and this dude is explaining everything in Japanese and I'm trying to sing in Japanese and I can't seem to put my fingers in the right places. But after a while it started to sound better as he poured more glasses of shochu from his bottle, and then we ate some German potato salad and raw octopus and steamed okra with sesame seeds. Man, the food there really is tremendous.

And about that time, these two young dudes come over and start talking to me in Japanese. And I'm trying to read the sheet music and missing notes, but pretty soon we're all singing and they're pouring me shochu from their bottle and I'm like, You guys are the best! Seriously! What do you do? And they're like, We're gangsters! And I'm like, *Yakuza?* That's awesome! Do you have tattoos? And they're like, Do we ever! And they lifted up their shirts and had these elaborate full-back tattoos. I was like, Whoa, just like in the movies! You guys are the most bad-ass dudes ever! Want some potato salad? And so we had some potato salad and grilled sardines and these hot mochi rice fritters. The yakuza and I really appreciate good food.

Approximately six glasses of shochu later, the yakuza guys suddenly jumped up and said, Let's go to another bar! And I was like, I'm so there! So we hopped in a cab and rode to some hostess club. A hostess club's this place where pretty girls pour you drinks and pretend to like you. And this one hostess girl with extraordinarily large breasts and a tiny skirt came and sat right next to me, put her hand on my thigh, and said, "You're from America? I love America!" And I was like, "Me too! Let's fly there tonight! We can stay with my mom!" But before we went to America I really wanted to do some karaoke, so I said, Do you know that song about God in the toilet? And she was like, Do I ever!

The song's awesome, seriously. It's about some girl whose grandmother teaches her God's in the toilet bowl. I guess like the Tidy-Bowl Man. At least such is my understanding of the Japanese lyrics. And so the girl cleans the toilet, maybe because, why? God's stuck in there or something. Hell, I don't know. Then suddenly the grandmother dies. Is this not the greatest song ever? It's so popular in Japan, and the best part is it's arranged as an American country ballad. Like, "Oh granny says God's in the toilet, so gotta clean the toilet, oh no, granny's dead, well, still gotta clean that toilet." Okay, maybe you have to hear it, but anyway, this hostess girl and I sang it together and we sounded amazing.

About this time, the one yakuza guy takes my hand and puts it under his shirt and starts rubbing his back with my hand. And I'm all like, Dude, are you gay? And he's like, No, I just like the way this feels. And I said, Well fair enough, but that's pretty much my definition of gay. Fortunately or not, he seemed to lose interest after a while, so I went back to singing karaoke and having the hostess with enormous breasts pour me drinks while we made our vacation plans. It was very close to the perfect evening.

And then instantly it was really late. The other yakuza guy just kind of wasn't there anymore. Then the other customers weren't there. Like one of those sci-fi movies where aliens are snatching people up. Then even the other hostesses disappeared, until it was just me and the "I'm not gay but I like guys touching me" yakuza dude, who was passed out and drooling on himself, and this hostess girl with obviously fake boobs who suddenly looked a lot older than she did a couple hours ago. And that's when I knew it was time to leave. I have foresight like that. So I paid my portion of the bill, about sixty bucks, which wasn't too bad, considering.

That is, considering it was exactly what I had left in my wallet. So I stumbled out and realized I didn't even have money for a cab, so I just started walking. Which was also the moment I remembered I live four miles away. It was also insanely cold, but I figured it'd do me good to burn off some of the booze. Of course, that's four miles walking in a straight line, which was by then plainly impossible, so it worked out to more like six. Then after a while the sun came up and thawed me out, until I guess I found my apartment. And today, now that I've had some rice balls, a can of miso soup, and duct-taped my little table back together, I actually feel pretty good. I'm definitely gonna start working out tomorrow. Though tonight I might drop by that izakaya simply to say hi. And maybe have just one beer.

Getting a Japanese Scooter License

So I finally got a Japanese driver's license, which anyone who lives here for more than six months should really do. Well, okay, so it's a scooter license. Contrary to popular belief, this does not automatically make me gay. Hanging out in men's rooms is what did that. Because astride my Japanese moped, I'm easily as macho as that construction worker from The Village People, plus I have more chest hair. Man, I love that guy.

They say that life's a series of accidents waiting to happen. But hey, why wait? Get yourself a tiny scooter in a country where it rains all the time and hug the side of the road at nineteen mph. Ken Seeroi lives for danger. People say that. Or at least I do.

For such a safe country, it seems Japanese folks can't kill themselves quickly enough. Like I was in Shibuya Station two weekends ago after midnight, waiting for the last train. A guy in a suit was drunkenly rocking back and forth in front of me, like he's dreaming of falling into a nice, soft futon. I'm always super-careful when I'm on the platform, because it's dangerous, really, with all these trains coming in. I guess I should mention that I'd also had a couple of cocktails. But according to Japanese Wikipedia, no one's ever waited for the last train in Shibuya without being "drunk as a *tanuki*." Now, that's a true fact—you can look it up. I entered it myself. And I was kind of fixated on this guy, because I had one of those bad feelings that I sometimes get. Then as the train roared in, sure enough I saw him stumble and take a header for the tracks.

A lot of people don't know I have cat-like reflexes. But I do. Even cats are like, Wow, damn, that's pretty fast. Really it has nothing to do with my childhood years spent training as a Shaolin monk, although I can seriously walk the hell out of some rice paper. So as this businessman lurched off the platform, at the last possible second, I lunged at him, grabbed a big handful of suit, and yanked him back. The train rushed past his head. I was like, Wazaa! I save you with kung-fu! He just looked at me like, Who the hell are you? And I was like, Dude, what the eff? You almost died! Only I said it in Japanese, and then he looked sad. He just stared at his shoes, and suddenly I felt bad, because I'd saved his life only to hurt his feelings. Jeez, Japanese people are so sensitive.

"What the eff" is the equivalent Japanese phrase you can expect to hear from exactly everyone when you tell them you want to get a Japanese scooter. In the minds of the Japanese, riding a moped is on par with being a kamikaze pilot, only you look way gayer. Everyone was quick to tell me about friends who'd been vaporized by trucks. But I scoff at that, partly because I'm without fear. The other part is that there's nothing I fear more than being without coffee for a couple hours, and I seriously needed an easier way to get to Starbucks. So after riding my tiny Japanese bicycle for half an hour just to get a Venti soy latte, I went to the DMV.

In Japanese, they call a moped a *gentsuki*, which is good because it sounds less effeminate. And from what I could gather online, there was a book about the Japanese rules of the road available at the Department of Motor Vehicles. Unfortunately, the DMV happens to be stuck in about year 1972 and hasn't yet discovered the internet.

The DMV building is essentially a square version of the Death Star. Inside the enormous entrance lobby was a little Japanese lady sitting alone behind an information desk. She looked kind of forlorn. I know I can be rather intimidating, in a big and white way, so when I walked up I tried to use my smallest and cheeriest Japanese voice. I said, Excuse me, I'd like to get a gentsuki license. Might you tell me where one would find a driver's handbook? She just glared up at me and said, in English—We have no English help. That's when I realized she wasn't sitting; she was standing. Christ, she really was mighty tiny. So in an even smaller Japanese voice, I bent down and said, Okay, a book in Japanese is no problem.

Where might I obtain one?

She squinted at me and said again in English, We don't sell a book.

Then she thrust a sheet of paper at me with Japanese instructions for obtaining a gentsuki license. I thought, Isn't this kind of sending mixed messages—speaking in English and then handing me this sheet? But whatever. Then I noticed that with her tiny arm she was pointing to another counter, so I went that way. Two women were standing at attention behind the counter, waiting all day just to deny the existence of any book covering Japanese rules of the road. I was like, You mean the DMV has nothing to do with the rules of the road? And they looked at each other, like it was the first time anyone had ever thought to ask such a question. Maybe you should go to a bookstore, they said.

A small, black cloud formed over my head and I walked out of the DMV mumbling. As soon as the double doors closed behind me, I saw a Japanese policeman walking into the building. Suddenly I was like, Well, let's just see what this fool has to say on the matter. So I ran up behind him and said, Dude, really, is there no book for the rules of the road? Isn't this country a bit lacking in documentation? He turned around, looked me up and down, then out of the corner of his mouth said, Go around the corner. There's a driving school. They have a book.

I went around the corner.

I walked past the driving school three times before going in because I couldn't believe it wasn't a homeless shelter. It was easily the most ghetto place I've been in Japan, rivaled only by the *izakayas* in which I typically eat dinner. When I opened the door, a fat guy with sweated-out armpits jumped bolt upright behind a glass case. Papers and books were everywhere. He'd obviously been sleeping in his own filth. I was done with the pleasantries.

"Rules of the road book," I said.

"We have no book," he countered.

"I know you have it. A cop told me. I want it."

At which point he rummaged through the display case and finally produced a green pamphlet covered in Big Mac stains. "2000 yen," he said. I opened it and it even smelled like hamburger. There was a list of true/false questions written in Japanese, and below them, an English-esque translation. Here's the first one, and I swear to God I'm not making this up:

T/F: When operating. When making a operation plan. Because it has taken a feeling to that. It had better do operation the place, the place.

I looked up at him. You're fucking kidding me, right? Really? He just shrugged and looked away. I stared at him intently and he gazed out the window, like maybe there was going to be an eclipse or something. Reluctantly, I picked two 1,000 yen notes out of my wallet, handed them to him, and took that delicious-smelling book back to my place, my place.

I studied like crazy for about a week, because the test has 48 questions and you can only miss 3. To make matters worse, the DMV is only open on weekdays, and as I actually succeeded in getting yet another job here in Japan, I had to take a day off work. It sure is a lot of work to get a moped just so you can get flattened by a bus, but I was determined.

I spent so much time studying for the gentsuki test that I kind of overlooked one small detail, which was the entire licensing process. Like, I knew the test registration opened at 8:30, so just to be on the safe side, I got there at 8:15. Count on good ol' Seeroi to be the first one in line. With an easy stride, I breezed through the sliding doors, stopped, and promptly crapped my pants.

The entire population of Japan had decided to relocate to the DMV. Every kid, office lady, and grandpa had gotten up at dawn to go to there and stand in line for windows that weren't open. Even people who didn't need a license had gone to the DMV just to hang out. Everybody was filling out forms like mad. Now, whenever I see that, I reflexively know I also have to fill out forms like mad, so I started running around the entrance hall trying to find the right ones. Only I couldn't find them, because there's about a hundred different forms and everything's in Japanese. And for the first time in years, I wished for English. Then I felt guilty for wishing that. But I felt guilty in Japanese, so it was okay.

I'm pretty good with Japanese in bite-sized portions. I can mail a letter. I can order a pizza, but only thin crust since I can never remember the word for "thick." I once even went to the dentist. But in the middle of this ginormous room surrounded by posters in Japanese and signs in Japanese and everyone speaking Japanese and about a million forms, everything started to go black and rotate around me and I thought, The hell, I'll never manage this one. Might as well just go straight to Narita and airlift out. Then I looked at the form in my hand and I heard a voice. It said, Remember your training and trust your instincts. Use the form, Ken.

You know, any time you hear voices, you really shouldn't be allowed to get a motor vehicle license. I started to decipher what I needed to write. I asked a pretty girl for help and she said she'd be right back. Then she ran away. So I was like, okay, better find an ugly dude. I went up to the ugliest guy in the room and he told me "Just check all 'No,'" which was exactly the kind of easy answer I was looking for. I was like, Thanks a bunch, man, and have you heard about Proactiv? Just trying to be helpful. Then pretty soon I'd filled in all the necessary boxes and even some of the ones I shouldn't have, and got in line with everyone else.

Oh, one small piece of advice for anyone getting a Japanese driver's license, in addition to "be born in Japan." That is: be able to write your address freaking perfectly, because you're going to need to do it about a billion times. Every single form needs your name and address, so if you, like me, take about two minutes to write your own address, you'll be hating life. I have a really complicated address, seriously.

Somehow I managed to fill in all the right forms, pay some

cash, and fool the DMV into actually letting me take the test. At which point I was herded into a room with about 50 Japanese kids, all sixteen years old. Everybody got a test. And then there was me.

It was really a toss-up between taking the test in English— with its bizarre grammar—and taking it in Japanese—with its, well, Japanese. I eventually opted for English, because if I'm going to fail a test, at least I want to do so in my native language.

Practically though, this meant I'd singled myself out, which I hate to do. It's not like I don't already stand out. So the whole class had to wait for me, the white guy in the front row, while three Japanese ladies carried in the precious English version in a plastic bag. They unwrapped it and laid it in front of me. "Don't look," the one lady said in English. I glanced at the page and in about one second had read every question. Gotta love English. "I won't," I said.

To be honest, the gentsuki test is pretty damn hard. I still don't know if I'm supposed to slow down when I reach the top of a steep hill, or speed up. I mean, how fast am I going, how steep's the hill, and what's the visibility like? Seemed like there were numerous variables involved, but I put True, because blasting over top of a hill on a moped seemed like the greatest idea ever. But the question that really stumped me was the picture of a One-Way sign, facing left. It read:

T/F: This sign means the gentsuki can turn left.

Well, that was clearly False, because that sign means One-Way. Then I read it again, and I thought, Well, wait, that sign doesn't prohibit a scooter from turning left. It doesn't mean you *can't* turn left. So I erased it and put True.

After the test was done, I walked out in the lobby and was like, No, you fool. You should have marked False. You've just doomed yourself to a life of riding a one-speed *mamachari*. Then suddenly came the excited squeals of a dozen teenage girls as the overhead a scoreboard lit up with the numbers of the people who'd passed. My number was 0419. For some crazy reason, the numbers on the scoreboard were only 3-digit numbers. I was like, What's my number? 041 or 419? Am I even looking at the right number? Anyway, some of the digits were up there, so close enough, I figured.

The rest of the morning was taken up with eye tests, paying more money, getting pictures taken, and writing my address about a million more times. Then we sat in a classroom and listened to this retired guy tell us how not to get crushed by a minivan. Since he'd seen me do the English version of the test, he made it a special point to explain everything in Japanese to the whole class, then turn to me and say, in English, "Do you understand?" That made me feel special. We watched a video of people getting run over by tractor trailers. After it finished, he turned on the lights, looked at me and said, "Mister! Do you understand?" Really, some people.

Then we had lunch. Now, I've held licenses in four different U.S. states, and I don't recall the process ever taking more than a couple of hours, including waiting in terminally long lines. But amazingly the Japanese have managed to stretch it into a full day event. After lunch we were given one very special form. Whatever you do, the retired guy said in Japanese, don't make a mistake on this form. Then to me in English, "Do you understand?" I was like, Yeah, I understand you're a dick. I took the form and started to write with a vengeance.

I got two kanji in and effed it up. I completely omitted the left half of one character. Maybe I can sandwich it in there, I thought, but when I tried all the lines bled together, so I started retracing the strokes to make it clearer. Thirty seconds later the whole thing was a dark blob. Everyone else was already finished. I wanted to die.

The retired guy made me sit in the back of the class, then went out and got a new form and this very ancient Japanese lady who was probably his mother to sit beside me. "Write the first character," she said. "Very good. Now write the second one. Oh, very nice. Okay, let's do another one. Oh, *jyooouzu.*" I was like, Jeezus, grandma, I made a freaking mistake, okay?

I've already written my address a hundred times today. How do you think I even got to this point? But of course, it was my own fault for screwing up, so I didn't actually say anything. Plus she was a pretty sweet old bird.

After that ordeal, listening to more safety talks, paying more money, and filling out even more forms, we were led outside for a Safety Course, where we'd actually get to ride the prized gentuski. "Goodbye, Mister," said the old guy. "Practice your address more!" Everybody laughed. Oh, will you please go to hell. I smiled and waved thanks.

We filed outside. It was a beautiful, warm day, with a line of mopeds basking in the sun. Five instructors divided us into two groups, guys and girls, and gave us helmets and white gloves. They put me in the girl group. All of the girls giggled, like I'd just failed gym class. Two girls near me said, in English, "Hello. Where are you from?"

"America," I said.

"*Heeeey*. Do you know a famous person?"

I thought for a moment. No, actually, I don't. Like, I met Bill Clinton once, but that's probably pretty boring to a 16 year-old chick. And it's not like I actually know the guy.

"Sure," I said. "I had dinner with Michael Jackson."

"*Waa sugoi*," The cooed. "Michael! *Sugoi*!"

"Yeah," I said. "He has really small hands."

I've never ridden a moped before, which turned out to be an extremely good thing, because the course was boring as hell. We spent half an hour practicing getting it off and on the kickstand. I gazed at the warm mountains in the distance just filled with gentsuki-ridable roads. After an hour, we'd ridden in a straight line. Maybe I could steal a gentsuki and bust through the fence. At an hour and a half, we'd learned to go in a circle to the left. In my mind, I was half-way to the mountains with a horde of gentsuki instructors chasing me, when I heard a voice say, Well, that's it! You've all passed! And everybody stopped and took off their helmets and gloves and started saying "congratulations" to each other. I was like,

What? I still haven't learned to make a circle to the right.

So we went back inside and paid some more money. I think the whole thing came to about 80 bucks. Finally, I got to the last window and they presented me with a license that, if I showed it to you, you'd be like, "Wow, you look like you just spent a full day being humiliated by the Japanese DMV." That's what you'd say. The guy behind the window handed it to me and said, in English, "Good job." "Thanks," I said, "you too."

And that was that. I walked outside a free man. It was still a beautiful day. I am now licensed to ride a scooter of 50 cc's or less. I cannot carry passengers or transport loads that extend more than 1.5 meters on either side. But ride I can. Now all I need is a scooter.

My Japanese AIDS Test

I went to see the Japanese doctor last week, because I felt a bout of AIDS coming on. This happens a lot, so it's no big deal. The only problem was I'd recently moved, so now going to get my butt examined by Sensei Stinkfinger means an hour-long train ride. So inconvenient, really, all that medical stuff.

Aside from its distance from the hospital, I love my new place. The only thing is, it's small. I mean like Wizard of Oz small. Like living in the Lunar Module kind of small. But on the plus side, it's got everything necessary to sustain life, including a TV, microwave, and even a bathroom. Now, you might disagree, but I think getting a beer out of the fridge, nuking up a plate of edamame, and using the toilet all without leaving one's futon is the very definition of convenience. It even has a teeny sink and a toaster the size of an Easy-Bake oven, like in case I need to make some tiny cupcakes. You can never be too prepared.

I move about once a year, in a vain attempt to improve my living situation in Japan. It's all about the trade-offs. My last apartment had a nice big window, but a view of a brick wall. The place before that was a room in a beautiful wooden house, which was great until winter, when the wind came blasting through and the place turned into an igloo. For three months, I wore a stocking cap and slept in a parka. That really messes up your hair, let me tell you.

But the real reason I like my new place is that it's not steeped in perpetual darkness like a lot of Japanese apartments. Instead, it's bright 24-7. I'm way up on the seventh floor, where the sun pours in every morning, and the neon glow gently tucks me in at night. I really gotta get some curtains. Anyway, when I look out my window, I can even see a bit of greenery, which is refreshing, since sometimes Japan feels like it's molded out of pure concrete. You know, there's not a lot of nature, unless you live in some deluxe tower like Bruce Wayne or something with a rooftop garden, or maybe you're homeless and live in the bushes down by the river.

My eyesight's really amazing, so way off in the distance, just before the horizon drops below the curvature of the earth, I can see a small tree. Ah Japan, so much nature. One of my lady friends came by and was like, That's not a tree. It's the billboard for a novelty car air freshener. But I was like, Nuts to that, you don't possess my spectacular eyesight. It's definitely a tree. Remind me to buy some binoculars from the hundred-yen shop.

So although my vision exceeded expectations, my AIDS did not, and I went to the Japanese doctor. The dude's always smiling. I've no idea why. Probably he's on drugs. I know I'd be, if I had to butt-finger people all day. But I don't. Smile all the time, that is, because want to know what the symptoms of HIV are? Freaking everything. And since I'd had a dry cough for a full month, I knew I had the HIV, and just resigned myself to it. I looked it up online, and sure enough, right there on WebMD was all I needed to know. To be fair, this is about the tenth time I've had AIDS. You name a symptom, I've had it. Rash? AIDS. Night sweats? AIDS for sure. Itchy crotch? Yeah, that ain't good. All in all, given the option, dying's something I'd prefer to avoid. Just too dramatic.

When I finally got off at the station for the hospital, it was raining, so I had to go to Lawson and buy a cheap plastic umbrella. And even then my pants were soaked below the knee by the time I walked into the waiting room. But compared to the masses of the people huddled there, I looked like a prince. Jeez, there are some sick people in hospitals. Folks were in wheelchairs with IVs hanging out of their arms, an old lady was laying across three chairs moaning, and a girl was crumpled on the floor coughing. Sounds like tuberculosis to me, but that's just an educated guess. I watch a lot of doctor dramas.

I love going to the hospital here. You get to speak a ton of Japanese, and because of national health insurance, it's actually cheaper than a language class. The first thing they do is give you a form to fill out with all your information, and answer questions about your health. I've learned a ton of medical terminology this way. There are boxes to mark for nausea, dizziness, fever, all kinds of good stuff. I check them all. One can never be too careful.

The thing about doctors is, they're smart. And they know it, so they don't try to impress you by speaking English. Not like when I go to eat *oden* at that old wooden cart under the railroad tracks and the homeless guy dishing out fish cakes from month-old broth has to try out his English. The dude sleeps in a cardboard box by the river and only comes out at night to serve up terrifying things floating in a pot from the Meiji era, but he's gonna make sure I know that he knows how to say "egg" in English. Doctors aren't like that.

The first thing doctors say is "Japanese *daijyoubu?*" And as soon as I'm like "*daijyoubu,*" we're good to go. I get my free language class. I get to tell him all about my cough, and that time I had a rash, and my athlete's foot, and he has to listen and ask thoughtful questions. It's great. Then he looks in my ears and mouth and taps my chest. But the best part is all the tests.

Japanese people love measuring stuff. Anything they can put a number to, they're on that. Height, weight, blood, urine, x-rays, you name it, they want to poke and prod you for it. Now, you wouldn't think "pee in this cup" would be something you'd want to hear, but when it's in Japanese, suddenly it's the most pleasing sound ever. I don't know why. Probably because I'd had a ton of coffee.

The only part that stumped me was the x-ray. They made me stand in front of this screen with my arms over my head and then some Japanese technician in a control room mumbled something through a microphone I couldn't quite make out. But I caught the word "right." So I turned to the right. And he's like, No, turn right. So I was like okaaay ... and slowly turned right again. And he's like, No, the other right. And I said, Where the hell's that? You want me to turn left?

And he's like, No, right. So I turned right. And he's like, No, Right!

Now, I know right and left. I'll admit there's a lot of stuff I'm not great with–*haiiro* (gray) and *chairo* (brown)–I gave up trying to keep those two straight years ago, since they're both just shades of dirt, and need to be delisted as colors. But I've got right and left down rock solid. All I can think is maybe he means his right, or maybe he wants to see my right side so I should turn left. Or something. So I turned left. And he's like "Good. Now turn right again." So I turned left once more. With my arms up, it felt like the hokey-pokey. Eventually, he seemed happy and we got a bunch of nice pictures, so I went back to the doctor's little room.

The doctor had two PC screens, and showed me a bunch of numbers and pictures of my lungs and explained all about cholesterol and triglycerides in Japanese and I was like, Hmm, I see, do tell me more. Then we got into a pretty deep discussion about the role of potassium in the body and I felt like I was really getting my money's worth from this language lesson. So finally, I asked him about my AIDS.

He looked at the screens and his voice took serious tone. Mr. Seeroi, he said, it came back negative. And I was like, Negative, ah, jeez, wow. How long do I got? And he's like, No, negative's good. I just looked at him blankly and tried to process that. I said, So negative's the new positive? You should really go talk to the guy in the x-ray room. Anyway, he continued, you're fine, but you ought to watch your diet. Do you eat a lot of salty food? And I said, Hell yeah, ever since this latest bout of AIDS I've been going every other day to eat *oden* at this old wooden cart. He gave me that disapproving look old Japanese people are so adept at and said, Try to eat some fresh vegetables and legumes. And I was like, That's good advice. Thank you, Doctor. Definitely not telling this dude about my weekends of potato chips and malt liquor. Physicians can't handle that kind of stuff.

Even though I no longer had the HIV, I still had a pretty bad cough, so I figured I'd go with plan B—other good illnesses. I started going down the list with him: lung cancer, pneumonia, whooping cough...I really have a great Japanese medical vocabulary. Surely it's one of those. He stared at his desk for a minute and thought. "When did this begin?" he asked.

"About a month ago," I said.

"Anything changed in the last month?"

"No..." I lied.

"New job," he continued, "or going somewhere new, or doing something new?"

"Well," I said reluctantly, "I did move to a new apartment."

"Ah, that's probably it. Have you cleaned it yet?"

"Perish the thought," I said.

I don't see what good it does to have all that fancy hospital equipment if all you can come up with is, You're allergic to your apartment. But that and a shitty handshake was all I got, so I thanked him and went back to the waiting room. A nurse gave me a prescription for some cough syrup and led me to the checkout counter, where a smiling young cashier handed me a green plastic card, and pointed to a machine behind me. "Put in the card. Put in money," he said in Japanese. Easy as pie. The staff there really are very nice.

Sure enough, it turned out to be some sort of reverse ATM machine. I inserted the green card and the screen told me to stuff in a hundred and thirty bucks.

I did a quick mental calculation. That's about a month's worth of potato chips and malt liquor. But I figured it was worth it, since it included two hours of Japanese lessons and cured my AIDS. I fed in a pile of yen and out came a receipt. When I walked outside it'd stopped raining and I realized my pants had dried, so I just left the umbrella at the hospital and rode the train home. In the end, I got a diagnosis of "Clean your effing apartment." It's pretty grim news, but I'm coming to terms with it. Thank God I live in a tiny space capsule, and with five paper towels and an old sock can clean the whole place in ten minutes. Gotta love Japan.

One Very Small Japanese Motorcycle

Why is everything in Japan so freaking small? I really don't get it. Like, they say Japanese people are short, but they're really not. Sure, there're some grannies who could pass as Seven Dwarf number eight, but there's also plenty of folks around my height, and I'm six foot. Although I do wear a lot of vertical stripes, so maybe that makes me look taller, I don't know.

At any rate, I finally got a *gentsuki*, which is what we call a moped here in Japan. Only it's not like one of those Italian numbers that a sorority girl would ride around campus in a bikini top holding a cappuccino. It's a pretty manly machine, actually. That is, for a moped. If it were just twenty percent bigger, it would be bad-ass, it really would. Freaking Japan.

Japanese people like things that are small, crowded, or both, that's what I've concluded. They say they don't, but they really do. Like, I work in an office with about a hundred Japanese men and women. No cubicles, just long rows of desks pushed together so everybody can raise an eyebrow every time my chair squeaks or I scratch a random part of my anatomy. Now, as much as I like the whole Japanese teamwork thing, I like my own space more. And since we've got all these other rooms that are never used, I went to my Japanese boss and in my humblest Japanese manner said, *Sumimasen*, why don't we use some of these empty rooms? He glanced up at me with his mouth twisted like a sour fish. He does that a lot. He was like, *Dame*, which is Japanese for "no effing way," although in my head I always translate it as "daaaaamn," for some strange reason. Anyhow, I was like, Hasn't anyone ever told you that Japanese people don't say "no" directly? He thought for a moment, and then said, "No." Oh, he's very witty like that. I'll send you some links to websites about your culture, I said.

The next day I showed up to work on my gentsuki, and when I walked into the office it was like I was wearing a Hello Kitty suit. A hundred people just stared at me.

"What?" I said.

"Hey Ken," the guy across from me said, "You got a bike?" In Japan, they call a motorcycle a bike. It's crazy. What they call a bike, I've no idea.

"Sure did, Nishida-san. But remember, it's not 'Ken,'" I said. "It's 'Seeroi-san,' right? You know, we talked about this?" Since everybody else is on a strictly last-name basis, and I'm the only white guy in the place, I've developed something of a complex about my name.

"Hey everybody!" Nishida announced, "Kenny bought a scooter!" Well there goes that.

Then Maeda-san spoke up. "Ken, I saw you this morning!" Maeda is the girl who sits two desks down from me. She's got terrible teeth. "You got a Super Cub!" she cooed.

"Yes," I replied, "Mister Seeroi bought one last weekend."

"Hey everybody, Kenny bought a Super Cub!"

On the Japanese scale of one to Samurai, some things are more, well, Japanesey than others. Shinto shrines, tatami, ikebana? Solid tens. Chopsticks and ramen? Okay, they're from China, so they only get a six. Sushi, probably a nine. Think kendo and manga are emblematic of Japan? Try riding a Super Cub. Easily an eleven.

Every Japanese person knows the rattly sound of the Super Cub engine and the ka-chunk of its gear shift. Since Honda's made them for fifty years, you'd think that shifter would be a bit smoother by now, but no. That clatter drifts into summer windows with every passing mailman, newspaper guy, policeman, and soba delivery kid. The Super Cub is the most produced motor vehicle in the world, and it's ridden almost exclusively by men, for some manly reason. Like, everybody's uncle rides one. If you're Japanese and your uncle doesn't have one, you freaking buy him one. That's just the way it works.

To be honest, my experience with getting a scooter license had kind of bummed me out, with the whole Oh-you're-a-foreigner trip. The important people at the DMV spent a full day talking down to me in pidgin English and treating me like their shoe-shine boy. But all that changed once I started walking into dealerships with a pocketful of yen.

If you want to be treated like a human being in Japan, just go shopping for a used motorcycle. Used bike salesmen are the nicest guys in the entire freaking world. I went around town on my bicycle until I saw a Honda sign in front of a small garage packed full of motorcycles. Inside, a portly man was poking at an engine with a screwdriver. He stopped and wiped his hands on a rag.

Welcome, he said. I want a Super Cub, I said. I have three, he said, and can make you a deal. How much do you have to spend?

Now that's more like it. None of that *Ooo*, your Japanese is so *jyouzu* business. The moment I told him 800 bucks, he stopped seeing white and started seeing green. He explained every aspect of the Super Cub in such exquisite Japanese detail that I could've been the Emperor himself. The only time things got a little fuzzy was when I asked about the model year. And then he couldn't tell me. Maybe 2002. Or 2004. Or 1996. It seemed a little fishy, but then that's Japan, you know. Like I couldn't tell you what street I live on, since there isn't a street sign for miles. Actually, I've never known any of the streets I've lived on here. Somehow, you just get used to not knowing stuff.

I went to half a dozen dealerships, and everybody was awesome. They all treated me terrifically, calling me "Seeroi-san" and speaking Japanese like I was a normal adult. That's not always easy to get in Japan if you look white. Or black. Or brown. I finally went back to Mister Portly and he agreed to throw in a free helmet and a basket on the front, so I said "Okay, Super Cub me." Like maybe I could use the basket for grocery shopping or something.

The price rather coincidentally came to exactly 800 bucks, which seemed like a pretty excellent deal. I handed him a stack of yen and he took care of the registration. It was the easiest thing ever, like an anti-DMV. I'm all about the easy. Then he picked what looked like an old blue construction helmet off the shop floor and handed it to me. On the front, it had printed in English,

CAUTION. Zoku is not entitled to wear this han cup which is for riders having good taste and manners. EST. 1958.

I put it on. As I have both good taste and manners, I felt entitled to wear that han cup.

"How do I look?" I asked.

"Now sunglasses," he said.

"Okay, how about now?"

"There's a mirror over there."

I walked to the mirror and there was one of the Village People staring back at me. "That's kind of disturbing," I said.

"Eh, could be worse," he said.

For some dumb reason, I bought the bike on a Friday night, which meant to get it home, I had to learn to ride during rush-hour while looking like I should be singing YMCA. It didn't help that I'd worn a pink shirt with a wide open collar and white vertical stripes.

It didn't take me long to figure out the Super Cub isn't actually a scooter, but a tiny little motorcycle. See, with a scooter, to make it go, you just turn the hand grip. To make it not go, you use the brakes like a bicycle. Scooters are butt simple.

But the Super Cub? God knows where all the controls are. One brake is where your right hand is. Another brake is under your right foot. Where your left foot is, there's the gear shift. You have to press that in two different ways, and I can never remember either. And you have to let off the gas when you press it, and then for some reason the accelerator, brake, and turn signals are all in the same place, up at your right hand again. Meanwhile the left hand isn't doing diddly-squat, except trying not to honk the horn. It's like a bike designed by

Picasso. If it were a cat, it'd have its feet where its ears are, and a nose where the tail should be. It's complicated, is what I'm saying.

But traffic or not, I had to get home so I was like, Okay, let's do this shit. With the dealer watching, I put on my sunglasses and construction helmet, adjusted the mirrors, put a foot on what I thought was the brake, clicked on the turn signal, and slowly eased it into first gear. "Thanks, man," I yelled, and hit the accelerator. I'd actually done it—got a Japanese license, negotiated and purchased a motor vehicle. I was awesome.

Only nothing happened. The bike didn't move. I looked at Mister Portly. He looked at me. I turned the accelerator further and the engine whined, but still nothing happened.

"I think it's broken," I said.

"Try taking it off the kickstand," he said.

Once I got into traffic, things got a little, let's say, worse. Going 30 miles an hour felt like a hundred. The shocks were springy and the tires kept slipping into ruts. I was like, Okay first gear, second gear, all good, not too close to the curb, okay now third gear and, Aw crap! Did I just blow a stop sign? It doesn't help that instead of big signs that clearly say "Stop," Japan uses these things that look like tiny red yield signs with some crazy Japanese thing written on them. I've no idea what they say, so it seems more like a weak suggestion than an actual law. And while I was trying to puzzle that out, I started down a one-way street the wrong way. So I quickly pulled onto the sidewalk, but instead of the brake hit the accelerator and knocked over a potted plant. Well, no time to fix that, so I just kept rolling around the corner.

Within five minutes, I'd broken every rule of the road, plus a few nobody'd ever thought of. I hit the brake instead of the gear shifter and turned on the high beams when I meant to do the turn signals. I kept trying to make sense of all the knobs and switches and meanwhile got horribly lost. There's only about five street signs in the whole nation anyway. Finally, I came to a stoplight and managed to get the bike into neutral.

Whew, that was a relief. Then the light changed and I couldn't figure out how to get it into gear again and suddenly there was a line of cars in my rearview mirror. Oh, that's bad, I thought. So I slammed it into first and wrenched the hand grip. This had the unexpected consequence of making the front wheel part company with the earth's surface. And then several dozen Japanese people got the pleasure of watching a white guy in a pink shirt and construction helmet ride a screaming wheelie through an intersection. After that, I decided maybe I wouldn't use first gear any more.

If there's one thing about me, it's that I have really good balance. Ask anybody and they'll be like, "Ken Seeroi? You mean that guy with the really good balance? Yeah, I know him." That really helps in cornering. And there's only one word to describe the feeling of leaning into a turn on a tiny motorcycle in Japan: freaking awesome. I made a right and powered into the curve. Sweet. At least I could do that well. So I flipped a quick left and roared around the corner. People were checking me out, like who is that dude? I was like, yeah, Japanese people, how you like me now? They were pointing and waving; I couldn't believe it. I was like, man, I love this place. Then I noticed a car coming straight at me. That seemed kind of bad. Then another, and then a whole nation of tiny cars was in my lane coming toward me. I had a momentary epiphany regarding the gap between theory and practice. Which is to say that while I understood that we drive on the left in Japan, I'd clearly failed to apply this in any practical sense. A few inches from the oncoming traffic I swerved into a parking lot, stopped, and sat down shaking on a curb trying to figure out why I'd baked a batch of cookies in my pants.

This went on for about a week. Then things started to become a bit more second-nature, until at this point, I feel I am no longer a menace to society. I am reformed. Sure, I can't find my way back home from the supermarket and still don't know what most of the road signs mean, but I haven't been arrested or killed anyone either. So that pretty much meets my life goal of being just slightly above average. Come to think of it, it's probably a good thing that bike isn't any bigger.

Japan, Happiest Place on Earth

Well, I visited a Japanese elementary school this week and had lunch with the kids, which was some kind of sparrow egg stew or something. It didn't really agree with me, probably because I don't like gruel all that much. Of course, thinking about the main ingredient coming out of a sparrow did little to improve matters. Actually, I'm not all that crazy about kids either. And that triple combination created a powerful desire to locate a bathroom in a big way, so I ran down the hall, jumped in the stall, and was like, Oh Christ, where the hell's the toilet? Where the Throne of Glory was supposed to be was just a porcelain trough.

I don't know if you've used the bathroom much in Japan, but sometimes this happens, and it's never good. It's just not right to feed a guy stuff that greatly encourages him to use the toilet, and then not give him a toilet. You just have to squat, which takes a surprising amount of balance and thigh strength. Like, I'm sure the acrobats in Cirque de Soleil can manage okay, but for a former American whose idea of using the can includes a steaming mug of coffee and a solid wi-fi connection, this is not an acceptable situation. However, as I was all out of options, I set about doing my business like a caveman. And just then, I noticed this little framed poem on the wall in front of the trough, like someone's going to be crouching down there so long they actually get bored and need some reading material. Then they're like, Oh my, a lovely poem, how delightful. Japanese people are strangely thoughtful.

It read:

幸せはいつも自分の心が決める

Happiness is always something your own heart decides

Japanese people are super weird, actually. Even still, it seemed like a pretty fabulous idea, being happy that is, so when I trudged back to the classroom I resolved to be happy, no matter what. That lasted exactly about a minute.

When I walked in, the third-graders were eating their

porridge in silence, all looking like the class rabbit had just died a fiery death. So I decided to liven the place up with one of my hilarious jokes. If you take two birds from flock, what do you get? A chicken! See, there's this play on words in Japanese, where "two birds" sounds like "chicken," get it? It's funny, right? A chicken! Okay, actually it's not funny in Japanese either. Whatever, you could at least pretend to laugh. But instead everyone just stared at their porridge. And then the homeroom teacher started yelling at the kids with his brown, pockmarked face, telling them to smile and making them ask me questions.

So this one boy looks up at me, and he's about nine years old and he's got a mouth full of sparrow eggs and rice and he mumbles, "How many cavities do you have?" And bunches of rice are falling out of his mouth. Japanese kids love to talk with their mouths full. It's gross. I was like, Aw, chew with your mouth closed for Chrissakes, kid. Also, I really couldn't think of a decent response. So I said "Six." I don't know why. All the kids nodded thoughtfully. The teacher was pacing through the rows saying, "Ken-sensei came all the way from U.S.A.! You should ask him many questions!" You could see them all looking down and sweating hard, trying to think of something.

Eventually, this one terrified kid with watery eyes raised his little hand. Great, I thought, finally a question like, How big are American hamburgers? or, What kind of pets do Americans like? Or something. And he just looks at me like he's going to cry and says, "Do you have any regrets?" Totally did not see that coming. I was like, Whaa? How bad does your life have to suck at nine years old for that to be your question? Regrets? You mean like I wish I hadn't been out singing karaoke and drinking shochu until four this morning? You mean like I wish I'd stayed in bed and not come to your crummy school that doesn't even have a toilet? You mean that kind of regret? But what I actually said was, Yes, I wish I'd done my homework like a good boy when I was your age. I thought that was a pretty fabulous answer. I should be a child psychologist, really.

But I realized then that this little boy's happiness was not something he could just independently decide. He was a product of a zitty teacher, a second-rate school, and a few thousand years of Japanese culture. And actually, I was starting to suspect maybe I was too. Like, you ever notice it's a lot easier to be happy when the weather's sunny? You feel good, everyone else feels good, and pretty soon you're having a summertime barbecue in your backyard with fifty of your closest friends and it's midnight and the cops arrive to tell you to turn down the stereo again. Well, that's exactly what it's like in Japan, only it's not sunny and there's no yard, barbecue, or stereo. Just a bunch of people staring at their shoes in a daze, like zombies in a monsoon. But otherwise, pretty much the same.

Somehow Japanese people have managed to elevate looking bummed out to an art form. It's like this crazy mass hypnosis. Did you know the U.N. actually has something called the World Happiness Report? Yeah, me neither, but Denmark is killing it. Meanwhile, Japan is dangling below Turkmenistan. Seriously, I didn't even know that was a country.

But going home, crammed into a steamy train car with a hundred people, everybody sweating through their suits and typing on their phones like mad, I was trying to make my heart decide to be happy without much result. Nobody talking, nobody smiling; everybody just heading back to miniscule apartments for a bath and five hours of sleep before getting on the train again. On the plus side, I can now touch-type about 35 words per minute on my phone. My fingers have gotten super nimble. I guess I'm pretty happy about that.

And then at the next station, three *gaijin* women got on the train, all sounding like they were from Alabama. I was like, Whoa, fat broads who dress badly. But they were so full of energy, talking, laughing, oblivious. I tried to remember what that was like, talking openly with other people, surrounded by supportive, encouraging friends. Man, Americans can do anything. I had a vague memory of my former life. Hanging onto the train strap in my salaryman suit, I felt mixed emotions. At least, I think they were emotions. No, I'm pretty sure. At any rate, it was very confusing, is what I'm saying. And all that emoting was building up a powerful thirst.

So when I transferred at Shinjuku, I decided to head out of the station to this *izakaya* I'm crazy about and have a bite to eat and just one drink. Six beers later, I was laughing my ass off with a dozen people, telling them about my sparrow gruel lunch and the toilet that wasn't. The guy next to me turned out to be a professional guitarist, even though he looked like some homeless dude with stringy hair. So I said, If you can play it, I can sing it, which is exactly half true, and when he produced a guitar we sang this Okinawan number, followed by "Never Been to Me," which brought the house down. I sound so much like Charlene when I hit those high notes that it's scary. Really, trust me, it's terrifying. Then I decided to have another beer and suddenly realized that, all reports and observations to the contrary, at that moment, I was in the happiest place on earth. Man, I love Japan, sometimes.

The Japanese Rule of 7

Seven Things All Japanese Just Gotta Say

It was my very first week in Japan, and already I knew something funny was going on. I guess I'm a little astute like that. I had this epiphany on the second floor of a small shop in Azabu-juban, which is a rather upscale part of Tokyo, as I was having tea with an attractive young lady of my acquaintance. When she excused herself to use the facilities (we'd had about a pot of tea, after all), the waitress came hustling over.

"Hello," she said in English. I looked up and thought, Jeez, you've got a lot of earrings.

"Hey, how's it going?" I said.

"Where are you from?" She seemed pretty excited. I looked to see if my friend was coming back any time soon.

"How do you know I'm not from Japan?" I replied.

"Because you're not Japanese."

"Kind of circular reasoning, isn't it?"

"I'm sorry, what?"

"Never mind," I said. "Are *you* from Japan?"

"Of course!" she said. "Can't you tell?"

"I'm American, so no, actually."

"Can you drink green tea?" she asked.

"Like a boss. How 'bout you?"

"Of course! I'm Japanese."

"Oh, I forgot."

"Isn't it too bitter for you?" she asked. "Don't you want to put sugar in it?"

"Well, maybe some people do mix in sugar, or even milk."

"*Heeeeey*," she said, and her eyes lit up.

"But have you tried it with salt and pepper?" I asked. "It's really good like that."

"*Iyaaa, muri!*" she squealed. Well, I thought, at least I got her to speak some Japanese.

At the time, I naively believed this to be a random bit of

conversation. I can be so wrong. As the same pattern began to repeat itself hundreds and then thousands of times, I gradually realized I'd stumbled onto something far more...what's the word? Insidious? Dastardly? Fishy? Mmn, nah, that's not it. Anyway, far more something.

Between conspiracies, aliens, and God, pretty much all mysteries are solvable. Got a circle in your wheat field? That's aliens. Imploding sky scraper? Conspiracy. The toasty image of Jesus on your waffle? That'd be God.

Now, I don't want to insinuate there's a conspiracy in Japan, but let's just say sometimes things seem a little too "convenient." The deal is, if you look "foreign" (whatever that means; but apparently, like porn, one knows it when one sees it), then you'll hear the exact same phrases, often in the same order, from every single Japanese person. How's that even possible? Coincidence? I think not. Special classes? Induction camps? Conspiracy, that's what. Sorry, but it's the only answer.

See, God's a good explanation for big stuff, like where wind comes from and why zebras have stripes. But how Japanese speak to foreigners? Clearly out of his purvey. Logically then, we're left with only Aliens or Conspiracy. That's just deductive reasoning. Either way, I'm sleeping in a tinfoil hat. Ken Seeroi's all about safety, lemme tell you, although it's really hot in the summer, and makes your hair sweat like crazy. But I digress. Let's just say you're guaranteed to hear the following seven phrases like clockwork, usually in Japanese, except for Number 1.

A Checklist for Japanese People Speaking with "Foreigners"
  1. "Hello!"

Actually, this sounds a bit more like "*herroo*," but we'll let that slide for the moment. Just remember that when you go to France, you're expected to speak French; in Italy, Italian; and in Japan, English. Abide by that and everybody's happy. Never mind that half the foreign-looking people here don't even have English as their native language. Japanese folks can't wait to enthusiastically bust out this word when they see your big, round eyes, just in case you've forgotten how much you don't blend in. The irony is that native English speakers rarely actually say "hello." But perhaps "whuzzup" is a bit too difficult to pronounce.

2. "Where are you from?"

I usually get asked this question in Japanese, and have found it a great phrase for making folks feel a part of any group. Please don't hesitate to try this on your friends of other races. There's nothing impolite about it, because really, nobody who looks like *you* could possibly be from *here*.

The world's changing, of course, and Japan's no exception. These days an increasing number of Japanese people happen to be white, black, or something else altogether. You gotta envy their lives, getting to field this question on a daily basis. Just think of it...a white Japanese person? That's crazy. That's like a black Englishman. Whoa, impossible. What's next, Americans from Europe?

3. "Your Japanese is great."

Subtle power-trip or innocuous compliment? You decide. No really, every day, you decide. And there's pretty much no decent response to this one. Just last week, I walked into a boutique to look at some manly handbags and the moment I said *konnichiwa*, the salesman was like, Oooh, your Japanese is great. I was like, Really? From one word? Well, actually, my *konnichiwa* is pretty stunning, now that you mention it. And just wait till you get a hold of my *sayonara*.

4. "Have you been in Japan long?"

This comes either before or after Number 3, and they form a nice set. If you say you've been here a short time, then the proper response is: "Wow, and already your Japanese is so great." Alternately, if you say a long time, then: "Oh, so then you're married to a Japanese?" In either case, you should anticipate follow-up Question 4.5, "When are you going back home?" Clearly, this is not your home.

5. "What's your name?"

Ah, an old favorite. So, the reality is that when you're not around, Japanese people use last names. But the moment you enter the picture, they start calling you and each other by first names. The last-name thing is like a secret handshake, a sort of Japanese closed society, straight up Illuminati stuff. But when they meet you, because you look so "foreign," they just take your family name, ball it up, and roll it under the nearest train. You get called by your first name, and that's the way it is, Ken.

6. "You use chopsticks really well."

So the other day I was in a soba shop next to this wrinkly old couple who would not stop staring at me eating a bowl of noodles. Their table was only a foot away, and they were like a combined 300 years old and the old lady was freaking fixated on me. I was all like, Okay, just don't look at the old people and maybe they'll go away. But then this skeleton claw reached out and grabbed my arm and started shaking me, and an old witch voice said, *Heeey*, you can use chopsticks really well! I was like, Jeez old lady, lemme go! All that agedness is probably contagious. Plus, that's my chopstickin' arm. I need that. But to be fair, my chopstick skills are, in fact, first rate. You should see me with a spoon.

7. "Can you eat *natto*?"

Of all the foods in Japan, somehow *natto* has won the award for the strangest thing "foreigners" could ever stuff into their mouths. Not sea snails, raw horse, squid innards, or whatever *monjyayaki* is, but gooey beans. There's about a million things on the Japanese menu more terrifying than natto, but Japan has unanimously elected fermented beans as gaijin kryptonite. Even buying natto in the supermarket is embarrassing. I try to wait till there's nobody in line, and then it's like, Yeah, I'll uhh, take this Kit Kat bar, a fifth of whiskey, 12-pack of condoms, copy of Penthouse, two *tenga* and...umm, some natto. No, not that one, the one on the left. Yeah, just go ahead and put it in an opaque bag, would ya? Jeez, I've got a ton of Kit Kats and Penthouses.

Japanese people live for rules. And when they meet

"foreigners," the only rule is they've gotta cover all seven points as rapidly as possible, then dispense with your ass. For years, scholars have speculated that this may even be an obscure law or ancient Imperial edict. Recent research has also raised debate over the actual number of required questions and statements, with some putting the number as high as twenty. However, seven remains the agreed upon figure for working calculations. One could argue more or less, but let's not split hairs and go all into imaginary numbers. Suffice to say these seven are etched deeply into the Japanese DNA, which is, of course, scientifically different from your DNA.

The Japanese Rule of 7 is, by the way, the world's safest bar bet. Here's how to win a frosty, delicious beer: Just wait till you hear someone say "*herroo*," then immediately turn to the person on your left and say, Bet I can tell you six more things this fool's gonna say. They'll be like, No way. Boom, instant beer. You can even use it with Japanese folks themselves, since it's physically impossible for them to exercise restraint on the remaining six points, no matter how hard they try. You're simply a mouse sandwich in a roomful of cats.

You can even apply the Rule of 7 yourself, outside of Japan, with "foreigners" and others who don't physically resemble you. You're guaranteed to make friends of all races by commenting on how well they use the cutlery. Can they eat nachos? Wow, and they speak English so well. When will they return to "their country?"

But just one caveat for those already here: the next time you're in a smoky *izakaya* surrounded by a rafter of drunk salarymen (which is every day if you're me), try not to inadvertently blurt out the answers ahead of time. Maybe you didn't come to Japan to be everyone's private minstrel show, but hey, since you're already here and all, how 'bout just a bit of that ol' soft shoe? Picking you out of the crowd and running through these questions may be a Japanese person's only source of light in an otherwise dark life. Gotta let 'em have that.

Every night, across Japan, there are men in suits dragging themselves back to their housing projects. They'll open the door and hear, How was work today, dear? And reply, Ah, the boss chewed me a new asshole again. But guess what? On my way home I talked with a gaijin in the izakaya, and he speaks great Japanese, uses chopsticks, and can eat natto! That's wonderful, dear. See, I told you life was worth living. Now eat your squid innards and take a bath.

Yeah, given the options, maybe being the minstrel isn't all that bad.

My Very Brief Fight With a Yakuza

This is the story I don't want to tell, about my fight with a Japanese gangster, because it's so horrible. But I've held onto it too long already, so I'll just lay it out.

The night started out pretty much like every other, drinking with some random Japanese girl in Ikebukuro. What can I say, everybody's gotta have a hobby. Now, I've heard people say that Japan's expensive, but it's really not. Seriously. Like I'll tell you what Tony Robbins told me. I'm sure you know him—he's that dude about seven feet tall with hands like baseball gloves. Sometimes I lie on the floor and watch him on YouTube when it's two a.m. and I can't stand any more Japanese TV. I'm not saying I even like the guy all that much, but from a Japanese perspective, he's amazing. He occupies an opposite universe, where people are huge and loud and can accomplish anything they put their minds to, like improving relationships and being healthy and successful. And I'm like, Hell yeah! I *can* take control of my life! I'll just finish this bottle of Sapporo, then I'm on it!

So lying there with my laptop on my stomach, Tony Robbins said to me, "If you do the right thing at the wrong time, you don't get rewarded. You get pain." And I was like, Dude, that is so true. That's like if you go to a "snack bar" with a cover charge and buy one beer and then leave. That beer's going to cost you thirty bucks. See, that's the kind of pain Tony Robbins and I know about. People who do stuff like that think Japan's expensive. But...if you go to a *nomihoudai*, you can drink all you want for two hours for about fifteen bucks. A couple of hours, are you kidding me? I can power down a good twelve beers in that time, and that's such a deal. Japan's cheap if you follow the right program. Anyway, that's what Tony and I think.

But where was I? Oh yeah, so that night I went with a lady friend to this *nomihoudai*, which by the way translates to "two hours during which you and everyone else will look way more attractive than they actually are." And we had a completely fantastic time, eating sliced tomato salad and octopus in wasabi and these mind-blowing *shiso* and *umeboshi* sushi rolls. But as it was Wednesday and we had to get up the next day for stupid work, we just said goodnight, bowed at each other, and went our separate ways.

It was a hot night, and when I walked down the steps into the station, even hotter air rushed up to meet me. Ikebukuro station is a sweltering, foul-smelling place. Then, near the ticket machines, is where it happened. I heard a loud thud, like a soccer ball being punted. I heard it again, then again. To my left a crowd of Japanese people were ringed in a large circle, and in the middle, a skinny man in a purple shirt was lying face up, unconscious on the white tile floor. Over him stood a huge guy with a shaved head in a cream-colored jacket. The big guy drew back his foot like he was going to kick a field goal—he had on these leather shoes—and booted the unconscious man as hard as he could in the ribs. Then again in the neck. He kept doing it over and over. The sound was horrible. Around him, nobody said a word.

I really couldn't process what I was seeing. Like, a couple of minutes ago I was having a bunch of nice drinks with this chick, and now it's like, What the hell's going on? Why is nobody doing anything? Where are the cops? Ikebukuro has a ton of police. People were just cringing, looking away, but not moving, screaming, or even speaking. Now, I try not to impose American values on Japan. It's another culture, like I get that. But if there's one rule about fighting, it's that you don't kick a man when he's down. No matter where in the world you are, that would seem to make sense. You certainly don't keep pounding on a guy after he's unconscious. And in the States, if someone's being attacked, you're supposed to help. At least you'd call 911 on your iPhone. Or take a video with your iPad. Or chuck your MacBook Air at him like a Frisbee. You'd definitely do something with Apple, for Chrissakes.

Like I said, so the skinny guy on the tile floor isn't moving and this massive dude is just kicking the shit out of him. And I know immediately the big guy isn't simply an ordinary person. He's a yakuza. I know these guys because they have a meeting every Tuesday morning in my town, in front of 7-Eleven. It sounds strange, I know, but maybe they just like the rice balls there or something. They are really good, actually. All these black cars line up with little old gangster guys sitting in the back, while muscly men in black suits mill around outside looking like K-1 fighters, with shaved heads and pounded up faces. This dude was one of them.

Everything happened really fast. I don't think I'd even been there five seconds. I was still trying to make sense of the whole scene. Plus I'd had a few cocktails. Then the yakuza dude did something I still can't deal with. He reached down and grabbed the unconscious man by the hair and lifted him up with one hand, until he was like a marionette dangling in the air. I just remember that purple shirt. Then with the speed of a baseball pitcher, he drove forward and whipped the man's skull onto the tile floor as hard as he could. It was like an explosion. Jesus, there was blood everywhere. It wasn't anything like a fight; it was like something from a war movie. I was like, Holy crap, this is an actual murder. The man in the purple shirt lay there lifeless with his eyes rolled back in his head, not even breathing, while all his dark blood poured out onto the white tile.

If you think about it, you probably don't see a lot of blood very often. Like maybe emergency room workers or soldiers do, but ordinary folks just don't see massive amounts of blood in everyday life. It's surprisingly dark red. Yet somehow, the yakuza still wasn't finished. He leaned over and once more picked the man up by the hair, like a lifeless doll. Nobody moved. The entire Ikebukuro station went deathly silent. And then he hurled the man's head onto the tile again, as hard as he could. The sound was awful, just bone on rock. More blood came gushing out. I couldn't believe it. Then he reached down for him again. I stepped forward and shoved the yakuza in the chest.

Now, I'm not a particularly brave dude. Like if your baby's on fire, count on me to be the first guy to take off running down the street for the fire department. Those dudes are professionals; let them deal with it. They've got big trucks and water hoses and oxygen masks and stuff. Police have guns and clubs and handcuffs. Only right then, in Ikebukuro, there weren't any police. There wasn't even a lousy JR station attendant. Just hundreds of people watching and nobody was going to do jack shit. I stepped next to the unconscious man in the purple shirt, put my palm in the middle of the yakuza's chest, and shoved him back hard, without a word, mostly because I couldn't come up with anything to say. And until that point, I guess I didn't really realize just how big he was.

His eyes were wild with anger and I knew he was going to take my head off. The moment he looked at me, realized I'd gotten into something I couldn't talk my way out of. Still, I couldn't help but wonder, What Japanese phrase would be appropriate at this juncture? Like I can make a dentist's appointment or book a room at a hotel, but somehow this particular situation had never come up in language class. All those flash cards for nothing. He moved forward until we were standing about six inches apart, and I understood one thing: backing down was no longer an option. I pulled my hand back from his chest. I saw a look flash in his eyes that said, I'm gonna murder you. And then he did something I totally didn't expect. He lowered his gaze, nodded slightly, and raised his hand vertically; the Japanese version of "sorry to trouble you." Like he'd just stepped on my foot in the train. Then he walked past me, up the steps, and out of the station. Just like that.

Suddenly everybody was on the phone with someone, but for ten long minutes, nobody came. No police, no ambulance, nothing. I stood next to the lifeless man and counted the time on my watch. I knew there was a police box near the top of the stairs, but jeez, did I have to do everything myself? The crowd mostly hung around watching, in a loose circle around this dude and all his blood, except for two ladies and a man who knelt beside him and patted him like a dead puppy. Finally an ambulance crew arrived. When they strapped him to the stretcher, to my surprise, he let out a faint groan and I noticed he was breathing. The human body is remarkably resilient. As he was being carted off, the police finally arrived.

People started drifting away. One policeman asked a few casual questions of a couple people from the crowd, and jotted some notes in a notebook. I walked up.

"I saw the whole thing," I said.

The cop looked at me. "That's okay," he said, and turned away.

"I can identify the man who did this," I insisted.

"We'll take care of it."

"He's wearing a cream colored jacket, and he went that way. I know where you can find him Tuesday morning."

"That's okay," said the cop firmly. "We'll handle this." He turned his back and strode away.

And just like that, it was over. I looked around. There were a couple of girls hugging each other and crying. A large puddle of dark blood was still on the white tile. I stood there stunned for a few minutes. Then I left. I didn't know where else to go, so I went to Family Mart and bought a tallboy of strong grapefruit *chu-hi*. Then I rode the crowded train home and watched another Anthony Robbins video on the floor of my tiny apartment, but it didn't make me feel as good as before. I guess I still think of Japan as a safe place. I just won't be walking in front of that 7-Eleven any more.

One Startling Trip to America

There's only one word to describe my recent vacation to the U.S.: Oh...my...God. Ohmygod.

I went back for two weeks, or as we say in Japan, *a fortnight*. That's a long time when every waking moment is filled with The Horror. By which I mean that between jet lag and culture shock, I feel lucky to have made it back to Japan at all. When I finally stepped off the plane at Narita I teared up so much that I just hugged the first flight attendant I saw. She happened to be from Korean Air, but I figured, eh, close enough. They're very soft too, those Koreans.

Now don't get me wrong, I like the U.S. It's just so...how to put this...American. Not that that's a bad thing but damn, there's sure a lot of *gaijin*, and they're all huge and insist on speaking English. Very unsettling. And suddenly, the whole nation has tattoos. Since when did everyone start looking like prison inmates who spent too much time alone with a Bic pen? I felt like the only Japanese guy in the whole airport. But because I had half an hour until my connection, I stopped off at the Sky Lounge for a calming tonic. I ordered a nice, familiar Asahi beer, and instantly things got a bit better. Funny though, it tasted a bit off, so I figured I'd better have another one just to make sure. Four beers later, I finally read the fine print on the bottle: Brewed in Canada. Damn your cultural appropriation, Quebec.

Thus ensued a spiral of reverse culture shock. Starting with the fact that Americans smell funny, and I don't mean sweaty. That'd be one thing, but this is more like a floral bouquet. Every shampoo and soap and hair spray has some scent. There's a variety of odors even for *de*odorants. How's that even possible? Riding the shuttle bus at the airport was like hanging out with the Fruit of the Loom guys. At least in Japan, everybody just smells like grilled fish. Man, I get hungry just thinking about all those delicious Japanese folks on the train.

Then I stepped out of the airport, and boom, onto a piece

of gum—did you ever notice how much old gum there is on the sidewalk? It's a sea of black polka-dots. Who even chews that much gum? And why spit it out on the sidewalk? Makes no sense. When I showed people my pictures of Japan they were like, Wow, it's so clean. Why isn't there any litter? Now there's a strange question. Like why would there be litter? You mean people actually throw trash on the ground? That's nuts. Folks in Japan understand common courtesy. The proper thing to do is wait until no one's looking and then stuff it into someone else's bicycle basket. That's known as civic responsibility.

Now, you probably don't know this, but I eat out every meal. If you looked in my tiny Japanese fridge, you'd be like, Yo, where's all the food? I don't even use the little lightbulb anymore since there's nothing to see. Saves on electricity. It's not that I don't enjoy cooking, but hey, all that slicing and dicing, jeez. What a lot of work. Me wash potatoes? Please. I calculated that in my life I've eaten at 25,962 restaurants. Although I'm not real good with math, so maybe I forgot to carry a 1 or something, but a freaking lot of restaurants, is what I'm saying.

The thing about restaurants in the U.S. is that they *look* fabulous, but the food's straight out of Doctor Seuss. I went to this Pan Asian place first. The walls were cast in oblique lighting with bamboo plants in every corner and tables set with cloth napkins and extra forks and knives just in case you dropped one or two. By the way, where the hell's Pan Asia anyway? Judging from the cooks, I'm guessing somewhere near Mexico. Then it took about fifteen minutes to get my first beer. That's about fourteen and a half minutes longer than I'm accustomed to. In Japan, you just shout "*nama!*" and Sha-Zam, beer appears. It's freaking magical.

But apparently in Pan Asia, unlike real Asia, beer is brewed to order and all your food comes at the same time. I'd forgotten that Americans don't order little by little and share. You just get one giant plate of stuff and chow down until your stomach's the size of a Thanksgiving turkey. Maybe that's more efficient, I don't know. I got some scallop and arugula dish. According to the menu, it was "pan-crusted and seared, in an *uni* cream reduction with a red pepper emulsion and drizzled with raspberry coulis." I was like, Can't I just get some food? Oh, right. I'll shut up now and eat my emulsion.

The thing is, I eat scallops on a weekly basis in Japan. Some people go to church; I eat scallops. When the rapture comes, don't go crying to me because you didn't consume enough bivalve mollusks, is all I'm saying. But where was I? Oh yeah. What those big white fatty things floating in the uni reduction were, I've no idea. But those were not freaking scallops. The whole dish was uber-rich and mega-oily and super-sweet, and now I'm out of adjectives but anyway there sure was a lot of it. That set the tone for my entire visit. And now I'm fat. Your fault, America, not mine. Not mine.

Then the bill came and it was about fifty dollars a person, on top of which we had to leave a tip. It's no wonder Americans don't do much karaoke. They've got no money left after dinner. America berry, berry expensive country. Sorry, too racist? Heh, not if you live in Japan.

And then I went to the men's room. Hey, half a dozen Sky Lounge cocktails and a few more in Pan Asia and I was ready to explode. Now, I don't know if you know this, but Americans can't construct a toilet stall that comes all the way to the ground. Like you can actually see people's legs while they're doing Number Two. Jeezus, who wants to watch that? It's gross. In Japan, you may not always get a commode, but what you get is almost always clean and plus you have your own private little room. In the U.S., if you really gotta take a poo— seriously, my advice is just go out to the park and find a tall bush. Trust me on this. Take some toilet paper or use a bunny or something. They're gentle and fluffy. Anyway, Americans have the potty cleanliness of infants. Like, they say it's the greatest country on earth, but if your citizens can't lift the lid before making wee, you may want to reconsider your standard of measurement.

And then walking from the restaurant, I met a couple of nice ladies. They were dressed well and said they were from out of town, and I was like, Oh me too. The one lady had this Gucci-looking purse and said she only needed a dollar in order to get somewhere. There was something wrong with her car I was unable to fathom and for some reason she couldn't just go to the ATM. I was like, Uh, sorry, I have to cross the street now. And then that nice lady called me all sorts of horrible names. I was all, Well at least I don't have some godawful butterfly tattooed on my thigh. Bitch. Only I didn't actually say that because I'm from Japan and we're polite. Plus there's a lot of guns in the U.S. You never know when some fruit salad-smelling broad's packing heat and gonna blast your ass. Ken Seeroi takes no chances on vacation.

So let's just agree that no country's perfect. It helps to have perspective. Although a few things gave me The Fear, I also found a lot of good. Like America has a ton of nature. It's got trees and grass and space. There's actually room, and people hang out in parks and skateboard and play catch instead of spending all day shopping for seasonally-appropriate chopsticks to coordinate with their place mats. Best of all, Americans talk, a lot. They talk to each other, strangers, everyone. Man, it's gotta be easy to learn English with people being so chatty. And in many ways, they're more polite than Japanese folks. It's like the opposite of the restaurants. Japanese people *look* fabulously polite, but it's mostly just outward appearance. If the U.S. doesn't seem especially well-mannered, at least most people are clued-in enough not to swoon over foreigners who can use forks, eat spaghetti, and speak more than one language. Americans may be rough around the edges, but way down deep inside those marshmallow exteriors, there's a lot of genuinely nice people. I'll definitely go back. Say in about a year.

How Japan Made Me Gay

I have Japan to thank for making me gay. I'm pretty sure it did anyway, since it's fairly desiccated my mojo. I keep checking the mirror to make sure, and while I don't look a whole lot gayer than before, the evidence is certainly mounting. Like when I woke up this morning, instead of my usual manly breakfast of cold pizza, cold eggs, and cold coffee, I had a massive carton of yogurt, albeit one significantly past the expiration date. Man, that really does a number on the ol' digestive tract. And said number, specifically, would be two. Definitely shouldn't have gone running afterward. That was a painful last half-mile I won't soon forget.

I'm just glad my uncles aren't around to see what I've become. Thank God they all passed away years ago from a steady diet of bourbon and Lucky Strikes. Those tough bastards were models for how real, manly men live. Briefly.

Red flag number one has got to be my newfound fashion sense. I don't know what happened; it's like one day I just started being embarrassed when stumbling to the convenience store with a three-day beard and wrinkly t-shirt. Soon, I went from mocking Japanese guys with their coiffed hair and tiny purses to wondering how I could get my eyebrows to look that good. And then it wasn't enough to walk through Tokyo in battered flip flops and beer-stained cargo shorts. At least, I think that was beer. At any rate, these days I can't leave the house without looking in the mirror and wondering, do these socks and tight trousers actually *go*? Well, they're both white with blue stripes, so I guess it's okay. Trust me, you start thinking that way and you're on the express train to Gaysville.

Red flag number two is the number of men masturbating next to me in public restrooms. This is a weird Japanese thing, and I'm sorry to have to relay it, but it's definitely a thing. Like *chikan* on crowded trains and flashers in raincoats exposing themselves to schoolkids, some public freakiness just comes as part of this culture. Not saying it's right, only that folks here pretend not to notice things that in other countries would result in a group of hicks in tank tops jumping out of a Camaro and pummeling you with a two-by-four.

Like last week I got off the train and went straight to the bathroom because it was Tuesday. See, there's this *izakaya* near my work that does half-price beer on Tuesdays. So it's a sure bet that I go there every week, eat a dozen gyoza and drink as many ridiculously cheap beers as possible before getting on the train. Hey, it'd be a sin to pass up such a good deal. What can I say, I'm religious like that. And that guarantees by the time I get to my station I'm straight ready to explode. So I hustle to the toilet and as I'm doing my business this dude pulls up to the spot next to me and just starts hitting it.

Not hitting the urinal—I mean, *hitting it*. Like, I'm not looking or anything, but if you're a guy, you know there's a range of acceptable motion one can do while at a urinal. And it's a really freaking narrow range, because you don't want to give the impression you're hitting it. And this guy was way outside of the parameters. And when something like that happens, you're just gay by association. It's like being at a party when cops show up and start asking whose crack pipe this is. Hey, not mine, but apparently we all gotta go to jail. I assume I'm not the only one this happens to.

And if somebody walked into the bathroom at that exact moment, I'd be like, Hey no, I was just standing here because I slammed twelve beers and it takes me a full minute to drain Mr. Lizard...but not gay. Yeah, sure you're not.

If this was the first time it'd happened, maybe I could retain some semblance of manfulness. But it's like the fourth time. Ginza? Boom, some old guy holding his dick like a rocket. Asakusa? Some fat salaryman. Ikebukuro? This high school kid. It's crazy. I don't know what's up with Japanese people. It's not like there isn't a stall they could duck into for privacy. And I don't actually think it has anything to do with me, although one could hardly blame them since I do have really nice eyebrows and exceptionally tight trousers. Most of these guys were already getting busy before I got there. Nor did they stop when other dudes came in to take a leak. Something about the Japanese group culture just makes them, I don't know, want some company. I'm not hating on gay people at all either. If that's your thing, hey, find a closet or a forest or something and knock one out. But do you have to second-hand gay me? I was just hoping to stay straight a little longer, that's all.

But perhaps the biggest red flag is that I don't find Japanese women as sexy as I used to. Look, no one's more shocked by this than me. Not saying they're bad looking, just that their personalities leave—how to put this—something to be desired. Somehow they were supposed to be way better than the ladies I knew back home. Kind of like how New Coke should've been so much more delicious than regular Coke. It's like you take Coca-Cola, but you make it New—so now it's better, right? When is extra sweetness not an improvement?

But yesterday, as often happens, I was in an Irish bar with a pint of Guinness and a basket of fish and chips, conversating with this rather attractive Japanese gal. Everything was right in the universe.

"How're the fish and chips?" she asked. I looked at her in that tight top and said, "Mmm, not as good as you." To which she giggled, and then, just when I should've leaned in and made some witty and slightly flirty comment, I felt a sudden wave of, what? gayness? Strange, because all the girls here used to rank between 8 and 10 on the Seeroi Scale. But now my math's gone to hell, and I start thinking...hmm, heavily padded bra...glued-on eyelashes...lives in a condo with her mom and little brother...her hobby is shopping...personal statement's "I think dachshund is super *kawaii*"...I'll give her a point for having a cuter handbag than me, so then carry the 1 and that puts her at, oh, round up to 6. Suddenly I realize just how picky and jaded I've become. And then for some inane reason, I decide to actually continue with, what's that called? conversation? Never a good idea, seriously.

"So if you could accomplish anything in your life," I said, "what would it be?" I like to ask the big questions, but that's just me.

"To be a bride," she replied without hesitation.

"Well, everyone's gotta have a goal. What does your boyfriend think?"

"Oh, I don't have a boyfriend. I just want to get married. To anyone."

"How ambitious of you. Well, good luck with that."

And right there, I knew. It was like someone pulled a Rock Hudson on me. The Old Ken would've had two more beers, turned that 6 into an 8, and made a night of it. But New Ken, ah jeez, he just had another beer and made for the door. Suddenly I began to worry it wasn't just mojo I'd lost in Japan, but something more. Maybe all that gay had rubbed off, so to speak. Eh well, when God closes a door, he opens a window. Or maybe a back door. Well either way, new horizons, I guess.

A Japanese Suicide

They say no one goes through life unscathed. But you know Ken Seeroi ain't trying to hear that. I figured hey, move to a nice safe country with pretty girls and amazing food and just avoid that whole scathing thing altogether.

Well, you can't say I didn't try. But instead, I found myself smack in the middle of something I was totally unprepared to deal with.

I met Shun and Makiko one morning as I was standing in front of my apartment drinking coffee and wondering what the hell I was doing with my life, teaching English in Japan. I do that a lot. Drink coffee and teach English, that is. It's a really bad habit. But somebody's gotta educate all those fucking kids. So when they came out of their place two doors down, they introduced themselves and we small-talked for a bit. Then they went to go clam digging, but not before inviting me to dinner that Friday night.

If you live in Japan, you know just how rare this is. I was like, holy shit, actual Japanese friends. People go decades without ever speaking to their neighbors, and to be invited into someone's home is nothing short of miraculous. I should also mention it's a lot more miraculous if you're speaking Japanese. People are way more willing to invite you over if you represent a free English lesson. That's a thirty-dollar value. But Shun and Makiko spoke zero English. God, I loved them.

Soon we were hanging out a couple times a week. I'd go over to their apartment for curry and beer, they'd come to mine for *shochu* and this desiccated octopus I buy at the convenience store. Hey, it tastes better than it sounds. Once in a while Shun and I would go out together and hit a cheap izakaya and talk about the kind of things Japanese guys talk about when women aren't around, like where you can buy Louis Vuitton bags that look just like the real thing for a fraction of the price. Girls can't tell the difference and they're such a deal. Shun and Makiko also had a two year-old daughter named Ai-chan, who used to scramble to high-five me every time we met. Unfortunately, Ai-chan also had a terminal case of snot emanating from her nostrils that seemed to coat her entire being, such that I was terrified of making any sort of physical contact with her.

Shun: "Ai-chan! It's Ken! Say hi!"

Ai Chan: Not a word, but massive amounts of nose snot.

Shun: "Ai-chan! Give Ken a high five!"

Ken: "Eeeeuuw, yeaaaah. Small...touch. Okay, good job, Ai-chan. And look, Uncle Ken's brought you a present! Your very own box of tissues! Here, give us a nice blow. Aw, Jesus, what're they feeding you?"

This went on for a few months, until I decided I ought to actually attempt cooking something in return for all the delicious food Makiko'd been making. I figured I'd invite them over the next time I ran into them. Only problem was, I didn't see them for a good three weeks. It was a bit concerning. We'd been planning to go to karaoke together. I even had a new song I was looking to bust out.

The crazy thing about my apartment at that time is that it had no furniture. None. Like, once I had a small table, but it self-exploded in the middle of the night. So I just sat on the floor with tall cans of beer and watched TV on the floor. It was okay. I have really low standards. And around midnight on a Saturday, just as I was wondering if it was worth crawling all the way to the fridge for another beer, the doorbell rang. I got up, put on pants, and there was Shun.

"Hey, how's it going?" I said. "Haven't seen you in a while!"

"Yeah," he said as he stepped in and took off his shoes. I could see something was wrong.

"I'll get you a beer," I said. "What's up?"

"You got the landlord's phone number?"

"Yeah, somewhere in this pile of papers. Grab some floor."

He sat down with his beer. "Where'd your little table go?" he asked. Then, "You seen Makiko lately?"

"No, why?" I said. "I haven't seen either of you in forever.

The table, uh, had to take a little trip. To heaven."

"I hope she's not dead," he said. He dialed the landlord. "He's not answering," he said.

"Well it's after midnight. Dead? Why, what? Why would she be dead?"

So it turned out they'd had a fight a week ago, and Shun had packed his bags and left for his mother's house. I was like, "Don't you have a key?" and he looked forlorn and said, "I was pissed, so I gave it back to her." Then apparently, little Ai-chan had been dropped off at her grandmother's house three days ago and no one had heard from Makiko since.

We went outside and looked at their door. "Maybe we could get in through the mailbox," I said. I'm real MacGyver like that. "Only all my coat hangers are plastic." "Doesn't it smell kind of funny?" Shun asked. We sniffed at the exhaust fan. "I dunno," I said, "maybe garbage or something." We went back to my place, then out to the balcony. He only lived two doors away. I stood up on my air-conditioning unit and looked around the partition. If you stepped onto the railing, you could hold onto the partition and swing over to the next apartment. Do that twice and you'd be there. I looked down four floors to the ground, and reflected on the small pile of beer cans I'd just drunk. It was really freaking high. "Maybe we should call the cops," I said, and stepped down. Shun got onto the air conditioner and stood there for a moment. There was a soft, warm breeze. Then without a word, he stepped onto the railing and balanced there. I thought it'd looked dicey before, but when I saw him up there it was way worse. If he fell, he'd be dead for sure. "Fuuuck, be careful," I said. I say a lot of dumb shit like that.

He twisted his body around the partition and dropped onto the next-door neighbor's porch, then began working his way onto his own balcony. It occurred to me that maybe the sliding glass door wouldn't even be open.

"Can you get in?" I yelled.

"Hang on," he said. "It's dark. I think I see her."

"Open the front door," I said. "When you get in, open the front door!"

I went inside, then out my own front door. In about one second, the door to Shun's place flew open and he fell out, screaming "She's dead! She's dead!" He dropped to the concrete as I caught him, saying "No, she can't be. How's that possible?" He was crying and shaking. "I thought she was asleep! She's cold, she's cold!" Holy shit, I thought. I held him in my arms and he wouldn't stop crying, just wailing. I was like, what do I say in Japanese? What would I even say in English? I know Japanese stuff like "Well, that's too bad," for when your bike gets a flat tire, or "I'm sorry to hear about your loss" for when your granny dies, but what do you say to a guy when his wife's just committed suicide? I said nothing.

Shun was babbling and almost incoherent, and suddenly seemed to be all wet, and I wondered if it was tears, sweat, or he'd peed himself. "Call the police," he said. I was shaking so badly I could hardly hold my phone.

"What's the number?" I stammered. "The number, what's the number?"

"110," he said, which in Japanese is pronounced a-hundred-and-ten. I knew that. I started to dial.

"Where the hell's the hundred button?" I cried. "I can't find the hundred button!" I was shaking like mad. Then I thought maybe I'd made a mistake in my Japanese, so I tried to calm down and check my numbers. Shun and I are splayed out on the ground, he's pale and wet and crying, I've got my left arm tightly around him and a phone in my right hand and I'm counting, One, two, three, four, five...until I get to eight and I still can't figure out where the hell the hundred button is, so I start over again, One, two three...

"I don't know how to dial the phone," I said. I pressed it into his hand, and he managed to get it dialed and passed it back. A police dispatcher answered. Suddenly, I didn't know what to say again.

"Hello," I said, "there's a dead person!"

"What's the person's name?" she asked. I couldn't remember, so I told her who I was. "What's your location?" she said. I couldn't remember.

"Japan," I said.

Shun and I were still laying there when the paramedics ran up the stairs, followed shortly by the police. Soon there was a swarm of stretchers, oxygen masks, medical bags, and police of every sort.

Unless you live near a row of bars, which I didn't, Japan's generally quiet at night. I could only imagine what the neighbors were thinking, with all the sirens and police and ambulance crews. A policeman squatted down beside us and started asking questions. This went on for about ten minutes, and I knew a solid million people in the neighboring apartments could hear every word. A lot of the questions were personal, and for the first time it occurred to me that this was a criminal investigation. I thought, shouldn't this be happening at the police station? Instead, we were just collapsed in a heap on the concrete. I was a mess. Shun was a disaster.

Finally I said, let's at least take this into my apartment. The policeman said nothing, but kept asking questions for another twenty minutes. Other cops came by and asked things. She'd been holding her phone and texting someone when she died. Who was that person? Where'd she gotten the pills she took? The ambulance crew went in and out and the medical examiner arrived to take away the body. I mentioned moving into my apartment again and finally the suggestion took. We'd been outside for nearly an hour, in a crumpled pile on the ground.

When we got inside, it occurred to me I had a different problem. My place was a holy mess. There were dishes in the sink and little stacks of garbage and empty beer cans, and everywhere were enormous piles of laundry. Hey, I was planning to tidy up on Sunday. Soon a dozen police were rotating in and out, asking every possible question of Shun and me. What time did Shun arrive? Why didn't he have a key?

How long had she been depressed? Was there infidelity? How had he broken into the apartment? How many beers had we had? This went on for hours, sitting on my floor.

Somewhere around four a.m. things got stranger. Makiko's parents showed up. Shun broke down when he saw them and with tears streaming down his face got on his hands and knees and bent his head to the ground, apologizing over and over. Her parents were crying. I was crying. The policeman was sitting there with his notebook and he was crying. I started madly stuffing laundry into the closet and put on some tea. I looked in my cabinet and all I could find was one tea cup, a plastic McDonald's glass, three wine glasses, and a Rirakuma coffee mug, so that's how everyone got their tea. Hey, I live by myself, what can I say?

Then Makiko's other children showed up. Other children? It seems she'd been married before and had two children, ages seven and twelve. They were bawling, having been awoken in the middle of the night to the news that their mother had killed herself. I gave them wineglasses full of tea. Shun's mother showed up. I gave her a beer mug full of tea.

Sometime after dawn, everyone left, except Shun, who asked if he could stay. We unfolded the futon and passed out. When I woke up a couple hours later, he was gone.

The next morning, I stepped out onto the porch. Christ, it was a beautiful day. This is where I'd met them a few months ago, and now Makiko was dead. I felt like hell. I decided to go for a run to clear my head. I went in and changed into a t-shirt and these short red running shorts, then went outside and laced up my shoes. The night before there'd been an emergency room's worth of medical devices on the porch, along with every type of police, fire, and ambulance personnel you'd ever imagined. Now it was all gone, except for a small flyer for a pizza place laying in front of the apartment where they used to live.

It was so strange. They'd cleaned everything up, except for this one ad for a pizza joint. I picked it up. I couldn't believe they'd never live there again. My friends were gone. For some strange reason, I tried the door handle and it turned. I opened the door.

Surprise party! Everyone was in the apartment! Hello! they all happily shouted at once, and Shun jumped up and ran to me. Come in, come in, he said. Holy Christ. I closed the door. Shun opened the door and grabbed me by the arm. Everyone's waiting for you, he said. Everyone was in black suits. I looked down and all I could see were my bare legs and these tiny red running shorts. I went in and everyone was smiling—have some food! Want something to drink? I was still holding the flyer for the pizza place, since I didn't have any pockets. I looked down again and to my shock, there was Makiko, lying dead on a futon in the middle of the room. Shouldn't the coroner have taken her away? Why the hell was she still there? She did not look very good.

"We're putting make-up on her now," said Makiko's mother. I'd never noticed how many earrings Makiko had before.

"That's, uh, good," I said. Again, I had no idea what to say.

Somehow, they'd run out in the early hours of the morning and already gotten a glossy 8-by-12 framed portrait of Makiko and laid it by her head, then whipped up a bowl of her favorite meat stew and placed it beside here, along with a bowl of rice. It wasn't even ten a.m. yet. A pair of chopsticks were sticking straight up from the rice.

"Come and sit beside her," said Shun. That was about the last thing I wanted to do, but as I had no choice, I knelt beside her dead body with my running shorts and pizza flyer and looked at her and her family, and wanted to cry. But since no one else was, I didn't. The whole thing was already weird enough. Everyone thanked me incessantly for the use of my apartment the previous night. After half an hour I made my goodbyes. I couldn't figure what else to do, so I went for a run by the river. Such a beautiful, sunny day.

Makiko's body lay there for another two days until they finally carried her away surrounded by flowers. Shun said he didn't sleep the entire time. He was wracked with guilt. He started cutting his arms with razor blades. He must have had a hundred cuts all up and down them.

Then on the third day they started cleaning the place out. They threw away everything, and I mean everything. Makiko's parents came by and gave me a case of Asahi beer. Shun gave me their microwave and a bunch of dishes, including some tea cups. I figured those would come in handy. It took them exactly two days to throw out all the furniture, appliances, and traces of life, then clean the place. After it was done, I went into the apartment and it looked like nothing had ever happened. All that remained was an enormous pile of junk in front of the building. No sentimentality, no mementos. They bagged up all of Makiko's clothes and possessions and laid them among the trash. And then it was like she'd never existed.

Who's Really Japanese?

When I first came to Japan, things were so much simpler. Men were men, Japanese were Japanese, and foreigners were *gaijin*. Now everything's gone to hell, nuanced to the point that when somebody talks about "the Japanese," I don't even know who they mean. I only know it isn't me. Things are complicated in modern Japan, is what I'm saying. Three things, specifically, or maybe four.

Thing 1: A Lot of Japanese Aren't Japanese

Literally, they're not. You know those polite Japanese welcoming you into shops and restaurants and bowing like crazy when you leave? And when you get home from vacation you tell your friends how wonderfully polite Japanese people are? Well, plenty aren't from Japan. As with service-sector positions the world over, they're frequently staffed by immigrants, meaning folks from China, Korea, the Philippines, even the Middle East. I met an Asian-looking Australian gal working as a waitress, who wore a kimono and let tourists take pictures of her, thinking she was Japanese. So polite, those Australians.

Now, if you know me, you know I eat out a lot, with "a lot" being synonymous with "every meal." And so I was in a restaurant a couple weeks ago, but no matter how many times I asked the waiter for some cold tofu, he just couldn't get what I was saying. See, I've been on something of a cold tofu diet lately—what can I say, it was a hot summer, plus I gotta watch my weight, since I eat out all the freaking time—and because I order it every day, I know my pronunciation's spot on.

"Do you have cold tofu?" I asked in Japanese.

"Oldofu?" the waiter replied with a Chinese accent.

"Uh, no. New dofu, but cold, as in chilled."

"Gold stove flue?"

"Cold tofu."

"Mold-toe shoe?"

"Yes, mold-toe shoe. That's what I'd like. Please bring me a steaming plate of mold-toe shoe."

Finally he disappeared and a Japanese person came and took my order. Damn foreigners, always messing up the place.

Thing Two: Books and Their Covers

You know how all Japanese people look alike? Well, my first job here was teaching English, and it was maddening, since all of my students looked exactly the same. I had four hundred adults who were like a race of clones. But as the months and years passed, I grew more accustomed to Japanese faces, and people started to look a little different. Then super different. Some had flat noses and narrow eyes, while others had high noses and rounded eyes. Some faces were fat, some gaunt, and they spanned every imaginable color. I even had one student who was bright orange. Gotta watch your beta carotene intake when that happens. All them cantaloupes and carrots really add up.

Anyway, after a couple of years, I started working with kids in the public schools. Now that'll expand your mind in a hurry. Kids all look completely different. Something about young people—you can see the genetics much more clearly, before they sit through years of mind-numbing classes that weather their faces into similar masks of boredom and resignation. A number of them obviously had various Asian, white, or black blood somewhere in their lineage, and a few were even whiter than I was, which is saying something.

Of course, the idea that all Japanese are Asian is as much a fiction as saying all Brits look like Prince Charles. I had several Japanese students who sported afros, others who were blond, and a couple with blue eyes. Quite a few weren't Asian at all. But somehow their outward whiteness or blackness failed to magically convey upon them the power of English. I'd be like, How's it going? and they'd tilt their heads and go, *Ehh?* They were less foreign than I'm Japanese.

Which brought up an interesting point. It's often said that Japan's a nation of one race, but the more I researched the subject, the murkier things became. Not only are there numerous races in Japan, but there seems to be no agreement upon the number of races in the world, or even what "race" is. The scientific consensus seems to be that race is an artificial construct, and doesn't actually exist in nature. This probably isn't news to anyone who didn't sleep through four years of high school Biology class, but it was to me, and might be to the majority of the Japanese population as well. It also turns out there's more genetic variation within races than between races, meaning that although I look as white as Eminem, I might actually be blacker than Chris Brown. Given that, you'd think I'd be a better dancer, but apparently there are some things science can't yet explain.

The clearest definition I was able to find divided the world into three races of people: Caucasian, Negroid, and Mongoloid. Where this leaves Mexican people, I've no idea. But I now understand the error I made. I thought I was a gaijin living among a nation of Japanese people, when in reality I'm a Caucasian surrounded by a bunch of Mongoloids. So I guess that's some comfort.

Perhaps a more compelling way of determining who's Japanese and who isn't is the concept of ethnicity, where members of a group are distinguished by their common language, background, culture, and ideals. While this sounds reasonable, I wonder how well it really works in practice. Like, I once met a dark-skinned black guy in an L.A. bookstore. He was college-aged, dressed in baggy jeans, Timberland boots, a jersey, baseball cap, and chains. He looked like a rapper. Yet he was fully engrossed in a Japanese software manual. I asked how it was he could read it, and in heavily-accented English he replied that he was Japanese. After being born and raised in Japan, he was now studying abroad. A lot of Japanese who don't fit the mold of "typical Japanese" seem to choose that option. Can't imagine why.

Now, I can easily accept the idea of a black man being ethnically Japanese. Because if he was born in Japan, what else could he be? But how does that play out for him here, when every time he enters a restaurant they hand him the English menu? Even fourth-generation Koreans get singled out as "not Japanese," despite having lived in Japan their entire lives and having ancestors from a country so close you could kayak there. The idea of ethnicity defining anyone as "Japanese" seems simplistic. Or is that idealistic? I really gotta save up for a dictionary.

Now, it doesn't take much imagination to see how quickly absolutes of nationalism, race, or ethnicity fall apart. In a world where you can fly Tokyo to San Francisco in nine hours and watch Simpsons reruns from your condo in Kyoto, boundaries frequently overlap and blur. If a child's born in Japan, but raised in the U.S., is that person Japanese or American? What if one parent is white, does that change the equation? Then take the opposite case: If a child's born in the U.S. but raised in Japan, is that child Japanese? What if both parents are Asian? Both white? If your cat has kittens in the oven, does that make them biscuits?

After visiting Japan a few times, I came back to the States and decided to enroll in a Japanese course at the local community college. I don't think it's possible to fit more geeks and weirdos into a single room. And in that group, two of my classmates identified as "Japanese." They grew up in the U.S., and in both cases, their grandparents had emigrated from Japan. They were third-generation Japanese-Americans, one had never even been to Japan, and both knew less about the language and culture than I did. Somehow they'd managed to be whiter than I was.

Similarly, one of my colleagues at a university here in Japan was a white man who'd been born in Tokyo, had a Japanese name, but had attended international schools and thus spoke only meager Japanese. He identified as American, despite having never lived there. So apparently it's possible to be born in a country, but not be of that country, and the reverse is also true. Maybe a diagram with some circles and arrows would help.

Thing Three: You Gotta Appreciate People Who Tell You the Truth

I met a rather "unique" individual in an izakaya a few months ago. And in the course of a conversation spanning several glasses of *shochu*, he informed me that a) he enjoys sex with transgender women, known in Japan as "new-half's," and b) Japanese people are terribly insecure about their racial identities. Frankly, you had me at transgender.

"Look," he said, "all Japanese people know their families originally came from places like China and Korea. We just deny it."

"Wait a minute," I said, "Go back to you to where sleep with women who are really men?"

"As long as they have breasts," he replied, "it's fine. I'm not gay, you know."

"Dude, if you say so. Anyway, China and Korea what?"

"And Southeast Asia, and Russia. Look, we all came here from somewhere. Only the natives of Hokkaido and Okinawa are really Japanese. And even they came here sometime in the past."

"I think we're out of shochu," I said. "So, like Americans and Native Americans, same thing."

"How else could we feel we're the only 'pure Japanese'?" he chuckled. "But try asking Japanese people where their families came from before Japan."

"Stop freaking me out," I said.

"You mean about Japan being a nation of immigrants?"

"No, you sleeping with women who are half dudes. Like, doesn't the plumbing get in the way?"

"Nah, they look just like women. You can't tell the difference. I'm not gay either."

"Yeah, and I'm not a *gaijin*."

As a general rule, I find people who tell you details of their sex lives to be people you can trust. Strange but true, and rare in this country. Understandably, Japanese folks don't like to have discussions about racial purity with individuals of other races, any more than white Americans would feel comfortable discussing "white purity" around black people. Still, I've broached the subject several times, and found conversations about "racially pure Japanese" (純粋日本人) to be fairly common. Japanese folks love to note which members of their group look more or less "Japanese." In talking with close friends, one thing's become crystal clear: preserving one's identity as a "real Japanese" is of the utmost importance. That, and the best way to do so is by labeling everybody else as *gaijin*. Okay, that's two things. Let's not get technical.

The truth is, as specious a concept as it is, race is everything in Japan. Japan's roughly where the U.S. was in the nineteen-fifties, with people of all skin colors making distinctions between "Japanese," "gaijin," and "other." It's similar to how "white" and "black" were much clearer in America before interracial marriages increased and suburban white kids discovered hip hop.

By contrast, consider this recent overseas headline:

Shouryya Ray, from Dresden, Germany, solved two
fundamental particle dynamics theories

The German teen solved a 300-year-old mathematical riddle posed by Sir Isaac Newton. Yeah, well sure, anyone could do that at sixteen. It's not like he's doing his own laundry. Only later in the article did it say that he'd arrived "from Calcutta four years ago without knowing any German." Yet despite growing up in India, recently moving from India, having an Indian name, and looking as far from Aryan as humanly possible, the article identified him as German. Well, sure. He lives in Germany. So, German. Another conundrum solved.

Now, grok on that for a moment. If Shouryya Ray had come to Japan, with his Indian name and looking all Indian and everything, then solved that theory, would anyone—even a single person—have said he was "Japanese"? Shaa, right. And why not?

In a word, race.

The standard retort seems to be, "Well, that's just Japan," followed a shrugged, "It's a different culture," and "Japan will never change." But really, it already has, and continues to do so at a fierce pace. You can see it walking down the street— from the Mongolian sumo wrestlers walking through Akihabara in massive kimonos, typing like mad with fat fingers on their Chinese-made American iPhones—to the legions of people lined up for a traditional Japanese lunch of McDonalds and Starbucks, to stores staffed by Japanese people from China. The nation's awash in foreigners and foreign culture even as it struggles to deny it. If Japan doesn't have a Rosa Parks moment, it's only because so few people actually want to be "real Japanese," with all the awkward social interactions and workaholic lifestyle it entails. But as the population ages and the world gets smaller, for better or worse, the notion of what it means to be "Japanese" continues to evolve. Sure, things never change. Until one day, when they suddenly do.

The Standing Bar, Some Karaoke, and 3 Beers I Never Drank

After teaching English at Bumfuck Community Center, I rode the train back into town and got off two stations early. Figured I'd walk the last couple miles home, get some exercise, and save a bit of money. Ken Seeroi, I said, you are one genius and healthy dude. I'd gone about fifty yards when I passed a standing bar. Well, that's enough exercise for one day.

The gal behind the counter handed me a large bottle of Kirin and a tiny glass. I carried them to a tall table in the middle of the room, near a young lady and her salaryman companion, who were busy in conversation. I poured the beer into the glass, watching as glistening droplets condensed on the outside. A perfect, creamy head formed on top. Ah, delicious beer. This is how I know God loves me. I raised the glass to my lips.

"Where are you from?" the young lady blurted out, looking past her companion. I set the beer down.

"I was raised on a ship," I said, "by pirates."

"What do you do in Japan?" she giggled. "Teach English?" We were now having a conversation around the salaryman, who was in the middle.

"No, our lunar module was supposed to land in Russia, but visibility was poor, so we touched down here."

She looked at me, batted her eyelashes, and said, "Do you like karaoke?"

I was like, "Yeah...," and then I heard a voice.

And the voice said, Ken, remember your training. There's something you used to do in this situation. What was it? Think, Ken, think. And finally I was like, oh yeah. I looked at my beer, then I looked at her. That body, those curves, man, how could I resist? That was one good looking bottle of Kirin. But since there's a lot of booze in the world, I reached past the guy, grabbed her by the hand, and we walked out the door. The salaryman just stood there open-mouthed, like What just happened?

Hey, when lightning strikes, you hit the jackpot, and the stars align, he who hesitates is lost. There's a lot of those expressions in English. Carpe diem. That's another. So we walked two doors down to a karaoke place, signed in, and had the guy at the counter send two beers up to our booth.

We didn't even make it to the first instrumental break before we were making out. I was actually mid-verse when I glanced up and she had *that look* and so the song went, "Imagine all the people, living for toda...ahh, fuck John Lennon," and away went the mike. A waiter came in with two beers on a tray, set them down, looked at us getting busy, then walked out with the same astonished look the salaryman had.

Now, people ask if Japanese girls are easy. Let me tell you, ordering a pizza is easy. Planting wheat, tomatoes, and basil, raising a cow for cheese, then fashioning clay into bricks for an oven to bake a deep-dish pie, yeah, not easy. Nothing's ever easy, because...why? I dunno. God hates me? Yeah, maybe, but at least he's inconsistent, so once in a while I get a break.

"Take me to your space ship," she whispered. I was like Say what? Oh right. I'd kind of forgotten about the whole astronaut thing. Anyway, she's got her arms around me, kissing my neck and I'm looking over her shoulder at these two golden beers on the table, just beyond arm's reach, all lonely and delicious. "Ah damn," I said, "let's get a cab."

The taxi dropped us off in front of Family Mart, right across from my apartment, so we picked up two cans of Asahi, a bottle of screw-top red wine, a container of potato salad, pack of cheese, some strips of dried salmon, a pickled radish, and two apple danishes. You can never be too prepared.

When we got up to my place, my mouth was parched and I was entering the late stages of dehydration. I was like, damnit, I *will* have a beer. I tore open the Family Mart bag, threw the food in the fridge, cracked open an Asahi, heard that old refreshing sound, and then "Ken..."

I turned around and was like, Whoa, where'd all your clothes go? She was laying naked on the bed. And I'm looking at the beer in my hand and I'm like, honestly, it's about 50-50 at this point. I flipped a coin, lost, and put the beer in the fridge.

Have you ever had sex when you're sober? Yeah, me neither. But you know, they say it's good to try new things in bed, so I figured I'd give it a shot. Can't say I'd recommend it though. Kind of like eating an unsalted pretzel. Like, it's still a pretzel, right, but just missing something, you know?

Afterwards, she turned to me and said, I have to go home, walk me to the station. And I was like, Oh, that's too bad, although it sounded like a quick way for me to finally enjoy a beverage in peace with some Netflix. So we walked hand-in-hand to the ticket gate, exchanged LINE info, and waved tearful goodbyes until she turned the corner and I ran to the nearest kiosk for a can of Suntory.

I carried that glorious tallboy outside and sat on the edge of a stone planter, near a small tree. Women walked by in short skirts and heels, long hair blowing in the breeze, but I barely saw them. You gotta have priorities and stay focused on what's really important in life. Man, there's nothing like a frosty beer at the end of a hard day.

How to Use Chopsticks

I'd been in Japan for almost a year before somebody finally gave me an honest answer.

Now going back in time, bit of history, I started using chopsticks when I was just a kid. I don't know why. It's not like my parents were secret ninjas or something. I guess I just like challenges, or possibly I'm retarded, but either way, I started using them at a super young age.

My recollection is mostly that I couldn't pick up shit and my hand hurt like crazy. But—and you know this is so me—once I made up my mind, I wasn't going to quit. Kind of like how I decided I would never speak English once I moved to Japan. And that's worked out just...uh, what's the opposite of "great"? Well, whatever, that's another story. Anyway, pretty soon I was this kid eating Cheerios with chopsticks, and Shake 'n Bake chicken, and meatloaf. Culinarily speaking, I had the whitest upbringing ever.

Ever try having Thanksgiving dinner with chopsticks? Cranberry sauce is super problematic. Not to mention pumpkin pie. But the amazing thing is that within about six months, using chopsticks became easier than a knife and fork. When you start eating Campbell's soup with them, you know you're making progress. Or you've lost your mind, or possibly both.

So I was in Yurakucho one late night grabbing a bite to eat with a Japanese friend named Masato. I call him "To" because it's easier to pronounce and sounds cooler than "Masa," which just reminds me of corn. And me and this dude go way back, so I can always count on him to give me straight answers. We ordered a couple bowls of ramen, along with every topping known to man. It probably goes without saying we'd had a few cocktails previously, thus ordering everything on the menu seemed a most excellent idea.

Now, you've probably read all the same things I have about using chopsticks. Don't use them to pass food. Don't leave

117

them sticking out of your rice. Reverse them when taking from a communal plate. A lot of it's pretty obvious if you think about it. Like in the West, you don't double dip chips or leave your fork sticking out of your mashed potatoes. Those aren't exactly "rules," so much as common sense. There's no rule that says you shouldn't put chopsticks in your ears and pretend you're a space alien either. Like, just think about things a bit, is what I'm saying. And yet, at that time, having been in Japan for less than a year, I was often worried about violating some sacred protocol, so I made it a point to ask Japanese people whenever I had a question about, well, pretty much anything.

Here's the thing about Japanese people: they love to tell you how to do stuff. When to put on your slippers, when to take them off, how to take a bath, the proper way to use toothpicks. Since it's their country, they automatically possess an expertise you don't, and damned if they're going to pass up the chance to display it. (This condition isn't unique to Japan, of course. I went to Texas and some guy in a diner delighted in explaining the proper way to eat chicken-fried steak. For some reason, gravy's very important to Texans.) But Japanese people, hell, they're the Energizer Bunnies of giving instructions. Case in point was this Japanese girlfriend I once had who told me—and seriously this is true—that I was putting on my socks the wrong way. Like maybe I was supposed to put on both at the same time? I don't know; never could figure it out. My next girlfriend told me I was applying conditioner to my hair all wrong and I clipped my fingernails too short. Another lady insisted I hold my umbrella a different way. Is it sexist to say that women in particular like to tell you how you're supposed to do everything? Okay, then I won't say that. Anyhow, a few months of this and I'd grown accustomed to thinking Japanese folks had some special method for everything, which I was dependent upon them to learn.

So when our ramen arrived with a mess of toppings—red ginger, bean sprouts, green spicy pickles, little rectangles of bamboo, and whole hard-boiled eggs—I did what I always did. I turned to To and asked for the procedure.

"Dude, are we supposed to use the plastic chopsticks or the disposable ones?" Then, as I noticed he'd already pulled apart the disposable ones, I followed suit. I probably don't need to say it, but for God's sake, don't rub your chopsticks together before using them. I've read that it would "offend the owner because it means you think his chopsticks are cheap." I don't know who came up with that bullshit, but the dude knows they cost one yen apiece, and he doesn't care. However, rubbing them together creates more splinters than it removes, and looks exactly as dorky as rubbing your knife and fork together before eating.

Then once I'd gotten the chopsticks apart, I figured I'd deal with the egg. "Is it okay to stab an egg with chopsticks?" I continued. Like, you're not supposed to spear your food, but jeez, it's pretty hard to pick up a whole egg floating in broth, you know.

"Mrmhmph," he said. "Sgrmrmph." I don't believe it's physically possible to have more noodles in one's mouth than To had right then.

"I'll take that as a yes," I said.

It was awfully good ramen, especially once one included every conceivable topping, plus a generous application of black pepper and sesame seeds. Then a new question popped into my mind.

"What about noodles? Is it okay to leave chopsticks sticking out of noodles?"

And here's when I got the first honest answer I'd ever received in Japan. Where every other Japanese person I'd ever met would have told me exactly what to do, accompanied by a mini lecture on Japanese customs, here's what Masato said, and it blew my mind:

"Do whatever you want. It's a free country."

That's it. Nothing about the importance of etiquette, or Japanese tradition, or how much of a foreigner I was. Just what

I would have said if somebody'd asked me which of the four forks to use at a fancy restaurant, or whether they should put ketchup on their hot dog.

Now, I don't mean to imply that there isn't a preferred way to do things. Maybe there is, but more to the point, really, who cares? Because there are two types of people in the world. And no, not "Japanese" and "gaijin." I mean people who tell you with grave earnestness why it's wrong to put your elbows on the table, and people who just freaking put their elbows on the table. In Japan, just like everywhere else, it's good to know which of those folks you're dealing with.

At the heart of this is a subtle fiction about Japan, repeated endlessly in articles and books. Japan's a nation apart, a sacred, mystical place with special rules and customs. It's not Japan the country, but "Japaaan," the fantasy combination of every Kung Fu rerun and Karate Kid aphorism you ever dreamed of. Writers describe Japan as a nation where people aren't absent-minded, they're "Zen-like." Articles on restaurants don't depict workers slaving away at menial jobs to pay their rent, but paint a picture of "dedicated employees striving for culinary transcendence." Japanese people don't take baths because they're dirty. They take baths to "purify their bodies." It's like some crazy app where you put in a normal activity and your iPhone converts it to a phrase from an invented, ancient samurai culture. You type in "bust ass," and it comes out as *ganbatte.* Well, I guess that does sound better, even if it means the same thing.

This idolization of Japan isn't limited to foreigners, of course. It's readily espoused by Japanese people themselves. "Japan's a nation that believes its own hype," a Japanese guy who'd lived abroad once told me. But maybe all places do, I don't know. Americans are convinced the U.S. is the greatest country on earth despite all evidence to the contrary. And Japanese people promote the notion that their country is a special place with unique customs that must be taught to Westerners. Now, I don't necessarily disagree with that. I just think sometimes they get a little carried away. Is it really important that I wear my bathrobe correctly? Apparently so. Seriously, try putting on a *yukata* the wrong way. They'll be on you like Godzilla on Tokyo.

The Japanese also have a saying that means "ignorance is bliss," only the literal translation is "ignorance is the Buddha." Jeez, even ignorance is more mystical in Japan. At any rate, I guess it's now my turn to play the Japanese guy and tell you the "right" way to use chopsticks. Ironic on several levels, admittedly.

So even after a lifetime of eating with sticks, I still got schooled on a couple of points that I've never heard mentioned in any "How to Use Chopsticks" guide. I'll pass them on to you, to save you similar embarrassment.

Thing One: Okay, this is minor, but you know those disposable chopsticks that come in a paper wrapper—the kind where you have to tear open the paper? Well, Japanese folks will always open that wrapper at the end that doesn't go into your mouth. They'll feel the wrapper and determine which end of the chopsticks are thinner, then open the opposite end. I don't even think most people are consciously aware they're doing this. So now you have a fun experiment to try. Give wrapped, disposable chopsticks to a Japanese person, and see what happens. Let me know. P.S. Don't hold disposable chopsticks vertically when you break them apart. It's not a rule or anything, but you look like a five year-old.

Thing Two: This is actually kind of important, so you may want to take note of it. See, before moving to Japan, I always just picked up my chopsticks with one hand and started using them, kind of like you'd do with a fork, but that's not "correct." Hey, what you do at a picnic is one thing, but if you find yourself in a nice restaurant, maybe you ought to know about this before getting schooled by your date. On the first date. Some women, honestly. Anyway, I'm told you're "supposed to" use two hands, in a three-step procedure.

1. Pick up the chopsticks with a soft overhand grip using the

fingers of your right hand

2. Carefully rest the tip of chopsticks on the index finger of your left hand

3. Delicately switch to an underhand grip by rotating your right hand palm-up, while still holding the chopsticks loosely with the fingers of your right hand

At which point you can begin inserting food into your pie hole.

And when you put them down, you do the same thing in reverse, using two hands. So there you go. Now you know some proper Japanese etiquette. For sure, it's good to know the right way to do things; just don't get all crazy and mystical about it. Japanese people break the "rules" all the time. And now that you know them, you can too. Happy eating. Or as we say in Japan, *Bon appetit.*

Winter in Japan? Balls, It's Cold

Wow, New Year's already? When did that happen? I'm still getting ready for the world to end in the year 2000 by backing up all my WordStar docs onto 5-1/4″ floppies and stockpiling canned *yakitori*. There's kind of this thing about time in Japan, where it always seems to pass faster than in the real world. And already it's been a rough start to the new year, since I showed up at work thinking it was Tuesday, when actually it was Monday. It doesn't help that Japanese days all have screwy names. Moon day, Fire day, Water day—jeez, how's a brother supposed to keep all that straight? I blame Google Calendar.

So I went to Hokkaido for New Year's again, and spent it with this lady friend of mine and her mom, real homey style, doing customary things like eating the giant box of *osechi* mystery foods and falling asleep on the floor. Actually, the falling asleep part is more my custom than a Japanese one, but after all that food and a couple big glasses of sake, hey, is it my fault I missed the countdown at midnight? Apparently, it is. Anyhow, there are only two places in Japan that are warm in the winter—Okinawa and Hokkaido.

Okinawa's like Hawaii, all blue seas and palm trees and stuff, while Hokkaido has mountains of snow higher than your head. Like it's eerie walking the streets because sometimes you can't see the cars from the sidewalk, the snowbanks are so high. Near the station they've got long red and white poles sticking way out of the ground, so you know where the sidewalk was before it got buried in an avalanche. Nobody wants you wandering off in a blizzard and getting eaten by a polar bear. Given that, you'd think Hokkaido would be really cold. Ah, but you'd be wrong. See, where homes in Tokyo are constructed with doghouse-like sturdiness, the northern part of the nation actually makes its buildings out of something other than single-pane windows and saltines. So as long as you're inside, it's warm, unlike my apartment, which was 9 degrees Celsius when I woke up this morning.

I don't know what that is in actual degrees, but it's freaking damned cold, I can tell you that. You know how Japanese people go to hot springs all the time? That's because the only way to keep warm is by staying underwater. Like maybe you could breathe through a bamboo reed or something. I spend a solid hour in the bathtub like that every night, then jump out and throw on a hoodie and socks and crawl into my futon, since unless I blast the heater constantly, the room reverts to the outside air temperature. Forget getting up to pee. There was ice on my door again this morning, on the inside. That's crazy. It's like living in a snow cave. I gotta say, don't move to Japan if you don't like winter, a lot.

And then there's Hokkaido. We went to this world-famous zoo. If you want to see a bunch of seriously cold animals, that's the place for you. The highlight was the lesser panda, which looks like a big panda, only much smaller. Actually, he looks like a little teddy bear. A really freaking cold little teddy bear freezing to death in the snow, but still cute. Oh, and the penguin parade, which is when all these penguins get together and walk through the snow. I guess that's kind of what it sounds like. Japanese people lose their minds for this sort of thing. Everyone was so busy snapping pictures with their smartphones, I'd be surprised if they saw penguin one. Probably the best part of the day for me was lunch, where we actually got to sit inside and eat hot food. I really liked that. Hokkaido has excellent curry, extra spicy and a bit sweet. It came with these terrifying fried shrimp with big-ass eyes that stared at me while I ate them. Maybe that part wasn't so great, but the curry was still delicious.

And later we went to the conveyor-belt sushi place and ate a pile of crab and scallops, which are really good because the ocean's so cold, or so I choose to believe. And then we went to the top of this pretty tall building and looked at tiny Sapporo down below and drank Sapporo beer. Then we came home and drank Asahi beer, which tastes exactly like Sapporo beer, only in a different can. Japan's fascinating in its diversity.

Well, I'm at work today, which is almost bearably warm if I wear a scarf and type with fingerless gloves, but since the day's almost done, I guess it's back to the freezing space capsule once again. Hope you're all having a great winter this new year, wherever you are. Hopefully somewhere warmer than Japan.

The Night My Building Exploded

So I was laying on the floor last night, actually trying to study Japanese, which is increasingly rare, since eating sashimi and drinking *shochu* with Japanese geezers at the local bar has replaced more formal study as of late. But, seeing as it's the new year and all, I thought I'd get off to a healthy start by cooking up an enormous cauldron of vegetable soup and doing something other than boozing. Yes, this is the year Ken Seeroi finally gets his life together in Japan. Plus it was raining, and anyway I blew all my yen drinking the night before.

Now, perhaps you're the kind of person who hears a lot of explosions, but I'm not. Like maybe a car crash or a big earthquake once in a while, but that's about it. So when this enormous, earth-shattering ka-boom shook the building, I thought, well, that's a bit odd. I'm calm like that. And then the fire alarm went off and I smelled smoke. I opened my window. It was still raining cats and dogs. The smoke smell got worse.

I live by three simple rules. Eat healthy, get plenty of exercise, and go to bed early. I don't follow any of them, but hey, they're still good rules. Oh, and Rule Four (a recent addition): Don't burn to death inside a Japanese apartment building. To hell with calm, it was time for a rapid late-night stroll. I grabbed my wallet, laptop, a hat, a pile of coins, a banana, and then I thought maybe I ought to stuff everything into a backpack, and then my phone, and my parka, a folding umbrella, and ran out the door. No keys. Where the hell are my keys? Crap, why can I never be more organized? The fire alarm seemed to be getting louder and louder. I rushed back in, decided to take some gloves, and my phone charger, and some Chapstick, and my passport, and finally found my keys and bolted for the staircase.

It was quite the scene outside. There was glass everywhere and half the neighborhood was huddled together under umbrellas. We looked up. A window on the third floor had blown to pieces. It must've been a hell of an explosion, because the window had been the Japanese version of safety glass, with wire mesh embedded in it, and now wire and glass were lying in large chunks all over the wet asphalt. The apartment where the window had been was dark. "He's dead," someone said.

That seemed a reasonable assumption, so we were pleasantly surprised when the front door of the apartment creaked open and one previously-dead neighbor stepped slowly onto the third-floor landing. The fire alarm was still ringing like mad. "It's okay," he called down, "you can go back in." He didn't look very okay. Then the door closed again. Nobody moved. A car drove by in the rain, over the glass. "That glass is really dangerous," someone said. "Yeah, that's a hazard," someone else said. Everyone agreed. That glass in the road sure was bad. Another car drove over it.

Okay, I get the whole Japanese thing, and try to fit in most of the time, but for Chrissakes, sometimes you just gotta be the white guy. I walked into the road holding my umbrella and slowly started sliding chunks of glass to the curb. Everybody watched. It took a couple of minutes, but I finally got all the major pieces safely out of the way. The fire alarm stopped. "Is the fire department coming?" someone asked. "Someone should call them," another person said. Everyone agreed they should come. I went back inside and up to the third floor, where I met another neighbor in front of his apartment. "Kerosene heater exploded," he said.

We use kerosene heaters a lot in Japan, because they're cheaper than running the apartment heating unit. I've never heard of one exploding before, but anytime you mix fire and flammable liquid, I guess that can happen. But hey, I'm not a scientist or anything. I use an electric heater.

Thirty minutes later, the fire department showed up. They didn't look like they'd rushed, jumping into boots and sliding down the fire pole, more like they'd just spent ten minutes in front of the mirror fixing their hair. Japanese guys, seriously. Then the police finally arrived, and the building management.

Then an ambulance crew. I went back outside. There were about a hundred emergency personnel with amazing hair ready to rescue someone, albeit half an hour late. I took a couple of pictures, then went in, ate some vegetable soup, spread out my futon, and fell asleep listening to the rain. It sure is a crazy country.

7 "Features" of Working in a Japanese Office

Somehow, things never work out like you think they should. Take for example, my plan, if you could call it that. I was working an office job in the U.S., and I concocted this great escape by which I'd run off to Japan and teach English to pretty girls for a year before settling into another "real job." Tangentially, the dream also included smuggling video games from Taiwan, drinking Asahi beer, eating cotton candy, and improving my tan. So why I chose Tokyo, God only knows. Hindsight, as they say, is a bitch. Or at least I say that. Either way, after a horrible year of teaching English, I somehow managed to interview and get high-paying office jobs in Tokyo, twice. I've got good credentials, so people often mistake me for being responsible and able to get stuff done. Hey, just because it says that on my resume doesn't make it true. And you know I was also pretty naïve at that time, because I thought there was nothing worse than teaching. So color me shocked when I learned that working in a Japanese office is like that musical with all the singing, fake French people–*miserable*.

Now, I know what you're thinking: "That's only two jobs," is what you think. That and, "Ken Seeroi, though brilliant and ruggedly handsome you may be, even you know that's not much of a sample size." Okay, good point, but hear me out. See, there are some things that are part and parcel of working for a Japanese firm, and if you plan on working here, you're gonna want to know them.

Job 1: The Small, Personal Company

So my first office job was a managerial position at this small company in a quiet Tokyo neighborhood. Real nice spot, with a park and trees and the whole bit. And on paper, the job looked great, because it came with a high salary and, well, okay, that's about it. But the pay was grand so, you know, gift horse and all. I bought a couple new suits and this excellent red tie I later lost in a karaoke booth. God, how I miss that tie.

Anyhow, on Day One they put me in this little room with two middle-aged Japanese ladies. One was my immediate supervisor. She sat behind me looking over my shoulder. She had a bald spot on the top of her head, so I figured that's why she was behind me. The other lady was my employee. I sat behind her, looking over her shoulder, although my hair is rich and luxurious. We did this for twelve hours a day. I drank a lot of coffee and constantly went to the bathroom.

Now generally, I'm a pretty positive guy, so I tried to fun things up right from the start. I figured we could use lunchtime to get to know each other, break the ice, do some team-building. Real corporate HR bullshit, just like in the training videos.

"Hey, so what's happening for lunch?" I asked. "All rightee, first day and all, how about we grab a bite at that café across from the park?"

"Gotta work," said Boss Lady, and kept on typing. Employee lady said nothing. She just looked at her hands.

"Well, okay," I ventured, "What say we order up a couple pizzas?"

Nobody said anything.

"I like mushrooms and green peppers," I ventured. "How 'bout you?" Boss Lady stopped typing. Until then, I hadn't noticed just how good the room's sound insulation was, but it was really quite excellent. "Although I'm open to anything," I continued. "Corn and mayonnaise? Octopus and broccoli? Sausage-lovers supreme?"

"I brought a *bento*," she said flatly. "Bento" is the Japanese word for a Tupperware full of cold rice, cold fish, cold boiled spinach, cold omelet, and a frozen meatball. Though it really tastes better than it sounds. She resumed typing.

"Me too," said Employee Lady. She still hadn't moved. I was beginning to suspect she had a disability.

"All right, well, tomorrow then, hey," I said enthusiastically.

"Working," said Boss Lady. Employee Lady sat like an ice sculpture, slowly melting into her chair.

So, having thus gotten to know each other, we worked another eight hours in silence in our little room, until it was dark and we all went home in turn: first Employee Lady, then me, and I guess at some point Boss Lady too, but maybe not. All I know is that at 8:30 p.m., I softly put on my coat, said a polite, "excuse me for leaving early," quietly walked out the door, then ran around the corner to the first bar I saw and promptly got plastered as hell. It was Monday. I lasted there seven months.

Job 2: The Big, Also Personal Company

The next place I worked was an enormous room full of people. I figured a large company might do the trick, with a good mix of foreigners and Japanese folks. The only problem working with Japanese people is they're about as fun as sofa cushions; and the only problem with foreign people is they're all weirdos. I don't mean that in a bad way. Okay, so I do, but if you live here, you know what I'm talking about. Being in Japan for a few years has a way of making one strange.

At lunch on my first day, I went to the "lunch corner" of our enormous room and sat balancing my bento on my knees, since there were no tables. Two white guys and a Japanese dude were doing the same thing.

"Hey, my name's Stephen," said this white guy named Stephen.

"Nice to meet you." I said. "Ken."

"You speak Japanese?" he asked.

"Yeah, pretty much."

"I passed the JLPT 2," he said. That's a language test foreigners think is important.

"Hey, great."

"I got 92% on it."

"Wooow," I said.

"Hi, I'm Randy," said this white guy named Randy.

"Ken," I said.

"You married? Got a girlfriend?" he asked.

"I'm kinda between situations right now," I answered, "if you know what I mean." Actually, I didn't even know what I meant, but it sounded like a reasonable answer.

"Yeah, I've got a few ladies myself. Check these out," he said, and proceeded to give me an iPhone tour of the women he was dating.

"Wooow," I said.

I looked at the Japanese guy. He nodded. "I'm Ken," I said. He nodded again, mumbled something into his rice, and kept on eating. Then we all went back to work for another eight hours. I lasted there six months.

Now, I know somebody out there likes their Japanese office job. People like snakes and spiders for pets too. Like, what about a puppy doesn't work for you? But that's cool, obviously everybody's different. I even dated this one girl who slept with a ferret in her bed. Damn furry thing kept waking me up all night. At least, I think that was the ferret. But where were we? Oh, yeah, so whether you like it or not, there are a few, uh, "features" that come with working in a Japanese office:

1. Expect to work a mind-blowing number of hours. Ever heard of work-life balance? That's because you're not Japanese. By law, hourly employees are entitled to paid overtime after 40 hours per week. To remedy this, the company will ask you to clock out at 5 p.m., and then to "voluntarily" continue working.

2. Forget cubicles. Get used to being surrounded by people that you try to ignore but are unable to. They in turn, will try to ignore you, only to be shocked when you blow your nose, look out the window, or breathe.

3. Are you a people person? Great, your co-workers will be incredibly friendly the first week. Then, having exhausted all possible conversation topics, you will sit in silence for the remaining years you work together.

4. You will learn to visualize success, as your boss, co-workers, and people you don't even know come to you with requests. Soon you will have such a huge number of miscellaneous tasks that you could only complete them by

working 100 hours a week. As people approach your desk holding documents, you will visualize successfully killing them with staplers, tape, and whiteboard markers.

5. High achiever? If you do an exceptional job, your boss and coworkers will hate you. Don't do that. On the other hand, if you fail to accomplish everything asked of you, you'll be considered a slouch for leaving before midnight. Learn what value lies in mediocrity.

6. When flu season comes, you'll be surprised how well you can recognize your coworkers from the different surgical masks they wear. Sick? No problem. Broke both legs and you're in an iron lung? That's fine, just wheel your bed next to your desk and somebody will prop you up so you can keep typing.

7. Like money? Bonus! As in, you'll get a bonus once a year, bringing your hourly wage to just slightly above that of a convenience store clerk. Want a raise? How 1990 of you. A decade from now, you'll still be making the same amount, unless the company does poorly and your salary goes down. Better work harder.

Now, I don't want to make it sound like working in a Japanese office is all bad. On the plus side, you're not in an Antarctic research station studying icicles. That's something. Depending on your workplace, you may have light, and heat. Those are good things, right? You may even have amenities like green tea, a coat rack, and a toilet seat that shoots water. You gotta learn to appreciate the small things in life, is all. But above all else, there is one priceless advantage of office work. Namely, that when you're in an Irish bar—and trust me, you will be—and everyone sizes you up as an English teacher, you can be like, Teacher? Huh, no way. I'm a *salaryman*. They'll all be like, Wooow. And that, perhaps, makes it all worthwhile.

On the Run From the Japanese Police

So last Wednesday I taught at this Japanese middle school. And as I was riding home on my midget scooter, I caught a glimpse of a Japanese motorcycle cop off to my left. I was cresting a small hill, and he was just kind of sitting there when I cruised past. I thought for a moment: Is this cause for concern? and then concluded, No, Ken Seeroi, you are a most excellent driver.

Sure, everyone says that, but I really am. I know this based upon the large number of cars, trucks, and bikes I've demolished. Well, maybe "demolished" is an overly strong verb. Let's just say "crashed," or "rendered unusable." That sounds a bit better. But really, let's say you're going into battle—who're you gonna want beside you in the trenches?—some pie-faced file clerk who's driven a desk the whole war, or a William Dafoe-looking dude all scarred and gnarly from scores of battles? That's the guy you'd want to ride with, right? Yet somehow when I explain this to women I meet in bars, they never get it. It's just simple logic, really. Anyway, I'm a good driver, is my point.

So I just kept going, winding down the hill and through the neighborhood. It was a mild spring day. The plum trees were dressed in white and red blossoms and birds were singing sweetly. Well, actually, there aren't a lot of birds in Japan, since about half the land mass has been replaced by concrete, but if there had been a bird, I'm sure it'd have been singing. Still, it was a nice day, and I was just glad to be out riding my little motorbike. Then from behind me, I heard a tiny woman's voice.

"Excuse me," said the voice, in Japanese. I looked over my shoulder and holy crap! there was an old lady riding behind me, on a scooter just like mine. It was like that weird dream where a witch is chasing you. I'm assuming I'm not the only one who has these.

"Excuse me," she said again. I couldn't freaking believe it—

an old Japanese lady on a scooter was trying to have a conversation with me. Or maybe she needed help. I stopped, because I'm chivalrous like that.

I quickly got off my scooter and went to see what was wrong. She met me half way. "Do you have a driver's license?" she asked.

"Yes, of course," I answered. What a weird old broad.

"Do you have a driver's license?" she asked again. Apparently this was a species of Japanese lady that says everything twice. I was tripping balls at this point, and then I noticed something and Boom! my head just exploded. She was like 70 years old, but she was wearing a costume. A police costume. The old lady and the motorcycle cop were the same person.

"I do," I said blankly. I was in shock.

"Do you have a license?" she asked again. That snapped me out of it. Lady, what the eff? Enough with the license already. What, a white man can't have a driver's license? And then it dawned on me. She actually wanted to see the thing. No sirens, no orders; this was police work in subtle Japanese style. And then I realized, she must've pulled me over because of my race. Because I'm white. I've heard stories about this.

I was not pleased. I got out my license and handed it to her. Racist. I said nothing. That's how you say you're mad in Japanese.

"Is this bike 50cc's?" she asked quietly, because my license only allows me to ride a tiny motorcycle.

"Yes," I responded. One word answer. Oh, I was telling her off good now, with my silence.

And then who comes around the corner but a dozen guys, my middle school students, and they all start shouting, "Seeroi Sensei! What'd you do? Are you being arrested?"

Oh man. "Not now, not now," I said. "Not a good time, guys." I tried to wave them off. No need to see your English teacher getting stopped for Driving While White. They erupted in a fit of giggles and promptly fell all over themselves hiding behind a stone wall. Then every few seconds a head or two would pop up and more giggling would ensue. Japanese kids are not very discreet.

"You know you ran a stop sign," said the old lady cop.

"You mean you didn't pull me over because I'm white?" almost poured out of my mouth. I let that sink in for a second, and then said, "Really? There was a stop sign?"

"At the top of the hill."

Oh, that's a little different. I mean, a stop sign, well. You'd have to pull over anybody who did that. Don't suppose it's too late to start acting nice. Perhaps a bit of the ol' Seeroi charm would be in order.

"It's just such nice weather we're having," I said. Then, "Aw jeez, I didn't see it! I'm terribly sorry!" I tried to look apologetic. "It won't happen again! I'm a teacher, you know. At the school here."

She wrote me a 5,000 yen ticket, which I had to sign. Bitch. "You can pay it at the post office," she said. She was fair and professional the entire time, which was unfortunate because I thought she might've cut a brother a little slack. But at least she didn't stoop to speaking English at me, for which I was thankful. "Be careful," she added. Actually, she was a pretty nice old lady. Still can't believe they let granny have a badge though.

So I rode straight to the post office while she flew away on her broomstick. The ticket was like 53 bucks, which is a pretty decent deal for completely blowing a stop sign right in front of a cop. Of course, the next day the whole school was abuzz with talk of how "Seeroi Sensei got arrested." Jeez, you'd think they'd never seen a white man get pulled over before. For next week's English class, I think it's time we learned the phrase "Fight the power."

Japan's Cat Islands

One fine Wednesday, I was walking by my neighborhood Cardboard Disposal Shed. That's the shed where you dispose of cardboard. Probably that's obvious, I don't know. But what's less obvious is this country's obsession with trash. You hear plenty about Japanese people being all into robots and jujitsu and origami, but almost nothing about the national pastime of sorting garbage into a dozen subcategories. It's like, what's your hobby? Really? Sleeping and sorting trash? How fascinating.

Sorry, where was I? Oh right. So it was a hot summer day, and as I'm walking by the cardboard shed, I hear this tiny meow. Only it was in Japanese, so it went *nyan*. And I was like, Whoa, there's a cat in the shed. So I slid open the door, and inside it was like an oven. And in the oven was a tiny black and white kitten. I said, How'd you get in here, and the kitten went *nyan*, and just then a much larger black and white cat jumped into the shed, grabbed the kitten in its mouth, and ran away with little *nyan*-cat. I thought, Damn, that's either its mother or one powerfully hungry cat.

On the door of the shed was a handwritten note in Japanese that read, "Please stop discarding your pets here." And next to the note, a full-color glossy poster with pictures of cats and dogs and an admonition to quit abandoning them. Which brought to mind the box of puppies somebody'd dropped off in front of my elementary school. Here, have some dogs—now they're your problem.

A lot of how you view Japan depends on your perspective. There are countless articles and videos describing Japan's amazing cat islands. Look at all the cute cats and kittens! It's feline nirvana. They spend days lounging in the sun by the docks, feasting on scraps the fishermen toss out.

Now, let's just be clear—*every* island in Japan's a cat island. You can't swing a cat in this nation without hitting, well, another cat. And the further south you go, the warmer the weather gets and the more cats multiply, until you get to Okinawa and you're positively awash in the critters.

Now, I love cats. Sure, they're heartless predators preying on local bird populations, but they're so darn cute. Lovely yet terrible. There's probably a comparison with Japanese girls that shouldn't be made here, so let's avoid it.

If there's one thing more heartless than cats, though, it's people. Literally every city park, every mountain trailhead, every dock you visit has newly abandoned kittens looking like, Wait, what just happened? Last week I was snuggled in a blanket and being fed tuna from a can, and now I'm in the fucking forest? What the hell? There's no food here.

Every night in the parks, there are cats, then more cats. It's an orgy of cats. They do nothing but sleep, kill things, and have sex. So just like people, is what I'm saying. Then even more cats. Cats, cats, cats. And then there are none. One night you'll be in on a bench drinking a beer, and suddenly think, That's strange. Where'd all the cats go?

Heaven, is where. Now, the alternative to culling are some trap-neuter-and-release programs, which "fix" the cats, then clip one ear into a *sakura* shape. That's great, I donate to these organizations, and hope they expand, because they're woefully few. And abandoned cats live a miserably hard life. They literally chew each other to pieces. Cats are cruel. I've seen so many dead cats in Japan, it's heartbreaking.

Viewed through this lens, the nationwide proliferation of "cat cafés" seems a twisted and unconscionable joke. Japanese folks stroll blindly past thousands of stray, discarded cats to then pay money for time in bright, clean rooms with cups of herb tea on little doilies, and cats. Really, this country, sometimes.

So the other day I visited an Italian couple. They'd just moved from Rome, with this cat named Palla. And Palla was truly a Roman statue of a cat, muscled, well-proportioned, just a beautiful striped tabby. Little tiny penis though. Funny about that.

And knowing the mangy, torn-up cats at the dock, I suggested, "You should probably keep Palla-san indoors."

"Oh, he's used to going out," they said cheerfully.

"Well," I said, trying to be gentle, "maybe not in Japan..."

"Ah, he'll be fine. He's a big boy."

I always try to be subtle. It's just that I suck at it, so I suddenly blurted out, "Japanese cats will murder your little tiny-penis cat." Kinda surprised myself, actually. Well, that rather killed the mood. But hey, somebody had to tell 'em.

I'm good friends with an American couple who took a different tack. They adopted a little black stray named Wedge, and took him out for walks on a leash. So that seemed an excellent compromise. Then they went a bit too far and taught Wedge to use the human toilet. Not sure how that benefits anybody. 'Cause he couldn't flush it with his little paws, so you'd go into their bathroom and there'd be these Wedge turds floating in the bowl. At least, I hope they were his. I decided to just pee in the potted plant on their balcony after that.

But here's how you know this couple's American and not Japanese: when they left the country (as *gaijin* do), they didn't just sneak little Wedge out to the park at midnight and go, Surprise! Call of the wild—see ya! Instead, they packed him up and moved him to Germany, which is where he lives now. Man, that's one lucky Japanese cat.

Smog Time in Japan

Ah, springtime in Japan; there's nothing like it. The world is once again alive with color as the *ume* trees bring forth their red blossoms, *sakura* bloom with pink, and half the nation is covered in a delicate, yellow smog from China. It is, as the Japanese say, a breathtaking sight. And God, nothing makes a man feel more alive than a city full of women in miniskirts, high boots, and white surgical masks.

I'm not sure what's happening to the earth, but I'm pretty sure it's not good. Between the desertification of Mongolia and the smogification of Beijing, the particulates carried on the high winds are turning Japan yellow. Not like it needs any help in that department. Every surface is blanketed in a fine, mustardy sand: cars, park benches, children. As a result, everyone's either sneezing, coughing, or wearing surgical masks, and usually all three.

So I came home yesterday wearing my mask, carrying a plastic bag full of malt liquor and tempura shrimp. Yo, Ken Seeroi's a great believer in maintaining a daily routine to maximize personal effectiveness.

This week, that routine includes opening a beer, microwaving as many snacks as possible, and finding the channel changer. I'm still working out the kinks, but so far it's been mighty effective. Only my pants seem to be shrinking, which I assume is a laundry issue. Is it my fault Japan has so many delicious snacks? No, it's not. I checked. And then, just as I settled onto a nice, soft floor with my fried shrimp and booze, I remembered, Damn, I forgot the laundry outside. For about half a week.

There's not much that's good about doing laundry in Japan, starting with the fact that the washers use only cold water. How am I supposed to get my whites their whitest? And then for some reason unexplainable in the Japanese language, instead of just throwing everything in a dryer and being done with it, the entire nation hangs its wash outdoors. Balconies and railings stretched from Osaka to the horizon are draped with everyone's long johns and futon covers. Unless it rains, and then everything gets hung indoors. On stormy days, my apartment's a dripping rainforest of wet clothes, with shirts pinned on curtain rods, pants thrown over the bathroom door, and a row of socks warming on the TV. It's damp, is what I'm saying.

So I went out on my balcony and brought everything in, then started folding and neatly putting things away. So much trouble, wearing clothes, really. Well, maybe "folding" is too precise a term. But somehow "cramming stuff in drawers" sounds worse. Maybe let's just say, umm, "compacting." I mean, I've got a tremendous number of shirts and there's not a lot of space in a Japanese apartment, even if one's clothes were folded.

I'd managed to get about sixteen white shirts wadded up and jammed into a drawer when I noticed, Hmmm, isn't everything—what's the word I'm looking for?—Yellow? Not quite. Orange? Eh, that'll do. I held a shirt up to the light, and turned it from side to side. You know how if you look at something one way, it seems messed up, but if you view it another way, it looks okay? Yeah, well, this wasn't that. No matter how I looked at the shirt, it had a faint orange glow. I guess that's an improvement, kind of. After all, orange shirt, what's not to like? But then there was the dust. My apartment smelled like a motor oil factory. I stopped the compacting process, sat there on the floor, and realized Japanese God was trying to tell me something. He said, Ken Seeroi, nature is vanishing, the planet is dying; it's up to you to do something. No one else possesses your special skillset. You are the last samurai. And at that moment, I realized He was right. So I opened a malt liquor, nuked up some shrimp, and turned on the TV. Gotta stick with the plan. Thanks, Japanese God.

Three cans of malt liquor later, I doused everything with bleach and stuffed it in the washer. Cost me six hundred yen just to get my shirts back to their original state, after which the inside of my apartment once again became a three-day showroom for wet laundry. But I felt good, because I knew that winter was finally over. That, and I'd had three malt liquors. Ah, soon it'll be time to relax outdoors, take in the wonders of nature on giant blue plastic sheets spread under the *sakura* trees, and remove our surgical masks to drink *sake*. Yes, spring is in the air. That, and just a bit more.

Sakura Ka-Boom

Another year, and already *sakura* season's almost over, thank God. So exhausting, all that relaxing under cherry blossom trees.

Sakura season isn't just great. It's better than great, whatever that is, since everyone's waited like six months for Japan to get warm again, and then once it does, Boom! it's *Hanami* Party Explosion. I guess I should note that *hanami* is the Japanese word for "sitting under blossoming trees on massive plastic sheets and drinking ridiculous amounts of booze while eating boxes of rice with little wieners shaped like octopuses in them." But *hanami* sounds more exotic, and anyway it's shorter.

On a related note, have you noticed that everything in Japan starts on April first, like a giant April Fool's joke the nation plays on its citizens? Schools commence, companies welcome new employees, and contracts are renewed. I finally figured out why.

See, if you had to face a year of working till midnight six days a week, and you got a contract in gray, freezing January, you'd say, Screw this, I'm moving to Vietnam. But in the springtime, when you see all those pink trees with their lovely cotton candy flowers, you think, Ahhh, Japan, how could I've ever doubted you? I love you. Now, where do I sign? Then a week later it rains and all the flowers are gone, and you're like, Aw, man, what've I done? Probably drank way too much sake, is what.

So once the flowers start to bloom, everyone and their employee races to the park to stake out the best spots under the flowering trees. And then the not-so-great spots next to the bushes. And then some rocky-ass ledge overlooking a canal, because you got there late. But you've only got a few days to get in your massive bacchanalia and then it's back to work for a year, so you invite everyone you know—come to my hanami!

147

My problem, as any doctor will tell you, is I have no self-control. I just cannot not go to every hanami party I'm invited to. It's genetic, so not my fault. Don't hate on the handicapped, is what I'm saying. So rather than lazily stumbling to the park in the sun with a couple cans of malt liquor and falling asleep on the children's play castle, I spend most of my hanami time hustling through train stations from one party to the next. There's a lot of flowers to see. Of course, they all look the same, but if I don't see them all, who will? I'm responsible like that.

So I'm rushing from one hanami to another, and it's hazardous, because Japanese people have an almost pathological lack of spatial awareness when they walk. Every day is like National Sleepwalking Day. And as I'm flying down the street on my bike to Ueno Park, this dude decides to step off the curb right in front of me. Not even a look before launching his body into the street. Good thing I wasn't drunk, because I swerved and just missed him. Probably should've snatched his man-purse and kept going, but I didn't because I'm responsible, like I said. Plus it was brown and I was wearing mostly black, so it wouldn't have matched. And this happens all the time, with people constantly making lefts, rights, and U-turns in the middle of crowds without once lifting their heads. I understand if you're texting on your iPhone, because hey, we all do that, but no smartphone equals no excuse, amigo. So buy one already. Anyhow, two hanamis and several cocktails later, I found myself running down the stairs to catch the train right next to some random dude.

Now, you're not supposed to run for the train. It's not, you know, like civically responsible. But let's be real—the next train's not for a whole minute and a half, and that's time you could spend assed-out under some cherry blossoms, so of course you're gonna run. And me and this guy are racing side by side to make the train before the doors close, going down the steps two at a time, and he's on the inside of the turn in front of me, so he jumps into the train first, and then—and this is so Japanese—just stops in the doorway, cold. Like he's instantly forgotten there's a huge white guy running full-speed an inch behind him.

Once we picked ourselves up off the floor, this is what our conversation would've sounded like in English:

"Dude, why the hell'd you stop in the middle of the doorway?"

"I didn't know you also wanted to get on the train!"

"What'd you think I was running for?"

"How should I know?"

But in Japanese, it sounded like, well, nothing, since we didn't say a word or look at each other. We just dusted ourselves off and pretended like nothing happened. Japanese unspoken communication. It's easier, sometimes.

My next hanami was in Yoyogi Park with a bunch of people from an English school I used to teach at. One of the dudes was dressed like a woman with a blue wig and voluptuous fake breasts. Actually, he looked pretty hot. We were in the middle of a long field and there was an enormous pile of garbage and at some point I looked up to see one of my female students squatting beside it taking a whiz. Ah, good times.

Hanami number five was a spontaneous one that happened as I was trying to walk through the swirling crowd of Japanese people making sudden turns in front of me. A group of college kids spotted me and yelled for me to sit on their blue plastic sheet. Actually, it may have been green, as my eyesight was starting to go by that point.

"Hey, come drink!" a couple of guys shouted in English.

"Okay!" I said, and sat on the edge of their sheet. I'm always up for new adventures of the liquid variety.

"Where are you from?" a girl asked, in English.

"Tokyo," I replied, in Japanese. Actually, it sounds kind of the same in both languages.

"No, where were you born?" she asked again.

"America," I confessed.

"Oooh," Everyone cooed. "America!" They always say that.

"Here, this is Japanese rice wine," said one of the guys, and poured me a paper cup.

"You mean, sake?" I said.

"Yes, rice wine," he continued. "And we say '*kanpai*!'"

"I see," I said. "How does one drink such a beverage?"

"Like this!" shouted another guy. "*Kanpai*!" and downed an entire cup.

"Well, fair enough," I said. "*Kanpai*!" and followed suit.

This seemed to make everyone quite pleased. We did it a few more times.

Suddenly it was early evening and I was in this little park near Oji, walking with some girl. The sun was setting. I remember she seemed very pretty and young, and we were walking slowly. I had a can of beer in one hand. I thought about holding her hand with the other. Since I had a free hand, you know.

"The trees are beautiful," I said. This is how you tell a girl you're in love with her in Japanese. You talk about nature.

"Yes, they are." she agreed.

"Spring is such a lovely season," I continued, "with all the flowers blooming and the air getting warmer. I wonder if it'll be a full moon tonight?" Talking about the moon is especially good.

"We should probably get back to the party now," she said.

Then suddenly it was two hours later and completely dark and cold. I was drunk as hell in some crowded urban park on the west side of Ikebukuro station. The lights were on under the trees and the flowers were all lit up pink. There was another woman beside me. She was older and had nice large breasts and I was crying for some reason. I was drinking a tall can of lemon *chu-hi*, which should've made me happy.

"It'll be okay," she said in Japanese, and handed me another tissue.

"But the sakura are all falling," I sobbed. "They're all blowing away in the wind. It's so sad."

"That's what they do," she said.

"But why does life have to be like this? Why does it have to be so tragic and so beautiful? Why does everything go away?"

"It'll be summer soon. You like summer."

"Yeah, I do. I really do. God, look at the petals in the wind—just like snow floating up to heaven."

"There they go," she said. "Isn't it wonderful?"

We sat there and she held my hand, the one without the chu-hi, and that's how hanami season went down, with the sakura scattering in the breeze.

Rock&Roll

So I was strolling down the *shoutengai* last Tuesday, which is what Japanese folks call a shopping street packed with rundown bars, vegetable stands, and stores full of granny blouses nobody ever buys. It was mid-morning and suddenly Rock&Roll-san veered into me on his rusty black bike. He was smashed. "Ken!" he shouted, "Let's get drinks!"

I was like, "Isn't 10 a.m. a little early for booze?" I try to wait until noon, as a general policy.

"I've been up all night," he said. "Let's mix it with coffee!"

Which is what we did. We went around the corner to this open-air bar where the bartender poured us two amazing espresso and cognac cocktails, plus cooked me up a grilled shrimp sandwich that took about half an hour to make. Like six tiny shrimp carefully arranged on a delicate bed of lettuce atop two thick toasted pieces of bread and creamy dressing. Now that's what I call breakfast, Egg McMuffin be damned.

I love Rock&Roll-san because he's a huge drunk, so we get along fabulously. I first met him at this *senbero* bar, which is one of those places you get three malt liquors and a deep-fried fish sausage for ten bucks. He had slicked-back hair and a leather jacket, kind of like a Japanese Fonzie. And the whole time he just kept belting out "Rock and roll!" which got a little old after a bit, so I left. Then I wandered through the *shoutengai* again before settling into another *senbero* place for three more drinks, and fuck me if he wasn't there too. So we sort of became friends out of necessity.

At some point, I'm sure he told me his name, but since we were always drinking there was no way I was gonna remember it, so I just called him Rock&Roll, which he seemed to enjoy.

Anyway, after that strong coffee and shrimp sandwich I was feeling pretty freaking energetic, so I said, Where to now? Fortunately, a couple of *senbero* places open at noon, so that was an easy answer. We dropped into the nearest spot and almost immediately a white guy sat down beside us. I was like,

Wow, *gaijin.*

I love gaijin, because they're amazing. So fresh off the boat, full of wonder and amazement. I guess that's all kind of the same thing, but whatever, the guy was totally cool, about twenty-three, and utterly clueless. He'd flown to Japan on a whim and somehow wandered himself into a local place with a menu full of stuff he couldn't read. I was like, Dude, you're me! It was like a trip back in time and meeting a younger version of myself, only without the amazing hair and fashion sense.

So I helped Gaijin-san order an obligatory three malt liquors and translated between him and Rock&Roll-san, whose only English was indeed "Rock and roll!" which he said at the least provocation. Well, at least you know what to expect, not like that girl Mariko, who demands I take her out and then always goes, "I don't know what I want to eat."

And I'm like, "How 'bout hamburger steak? You like hamburger steak." This is what Japanese people call a hamburger sitting on a plate with no bun.

And Mariko's all whiney like, "No, I don't want *thaat.*"

"Waffles? You're always saying you want waffles."

"No, not *waaffles.*"

"Well, Chinese? Thai? How 'bout curry? Fuck it, let's go get curry."

And when we get to the curry place, sit down and order, then she says, "I wanted *haamburger steeeak.*"

So Rock&Roll-san's not like that, is what I'm saying. As long as booze is flowing, he's happy as cherry pie. We've so much in common. Then after a bit, our merry band polished off the malt liquors, so we stumbled out to some white lawn chairs in front of this little shack selling cans of beer. There was an old geezer next to us speaking in local dialect, which Rock&Roll-san translated into Japanese and I then passed on to Gaijin-san in English.

"I lived through the war," said the old man in dialect, "and American soldiers gave me chocolate."

"He lives in a wall," said Rock&Roll-san to me, "and Amway sends him checks."

"He loves to wear fur," I translated, "and Armenians stole his pork chops."

"Bro," said Gaijin-san, "How'd you learn how to speak Japanese so well?'

"Years of practice," I replied.

So we powered down a few cans of beer till the sun started sinking and the sky turned all orange. Then Gaijin-san faded away to look for his hotel, Rock&Roll-san went off to work, and the old man went back to his wall. I called Mariko on the phone.

"Where've you been?" she demanded. "I'm *huungry*."

"Let's go get hamburger steak," I said.

"But I don't *waant* hamburger steak," she whined.

"Yeah you do," I said. "Trust me, you do."

What to Bring to Japan, an 8-Item Checklist

If you're planning to visit Japan, there's definitely some stuff you should and shouldn't bring. And moving to Japan? Whoa, then you really need to consider what to cram into your gym bag. But not to worry. As always, Ken Seeroi's here for you, doing all that pesky thinking so you can kick back with a margarita and relax. Here's all you really need to know.

1. Clothes

First, carefully select your best outfits and neatly pack them into two suitcases. Then put the suitcases into the trunk of your car and drive to the nearest forest. You'll also need a can of gasoline. Guess I forgot to mention that. Then once you get there, send your wardrobe to Fashion Heaven in a massive conflagration because no one in Japan wears that shit. This goes double if you're a guy. Japanese people place an insane amount of importance on personal appearance, and what's popular overseas is usually not popular here. So if you want to look good in Japan, buy clothes in Japan. Unless you've got some crazy size, like you're super fat or much over six feet tall, in which case, okay, you shouldn't have burned all your clothes. Sorry about that.

2. Shoes

Men six-foot-one or less won't have trouble finding things that fit, unless you're a big fat fatty. The same's probably true for women of average sizes, albeit my research is limited to rifling through your drawers and closets while you're in the shower. But shoes are another matter. Men's shoes top out at about US 10.5 or 11 in most stores, so if your feet are bigger, you're gonna need to bring shoes, and ones that match Japanese fashions. Yeah, I know, it's a conundrum.

3. Medicine?

Know how you can go to a 7-Eleven in the U.S. and get some Tylenol and Tums? Well, you can't do that in Japan. I don't know why. You can buy a fifth of whiskey, cigarettes, and the weak Japanese equivalent of *Playboy* twenty-four hours a day, but you can't get one freaking aspirin. You can get yourself into trouble, but you can't get yourself out. That's Japan for you.

Now, it's possible to go to a specialized "drug store" and get all that stuff, assuming its daytime. But for some sick reason, most places close at night, so when you wake up at 4 a.m. with a temperature of 42C, finding an open pharmacy's gonna be your personal hell on earth. But what are the chances you'll have a problem? It's not like you're eating unfamiliar foods from street vendors, drinking a pile of booze, and riding packed trains with ten thousand people who don't cover their mouths when they cough and sneeze. Let's just call that a Japanese "cultural" trait, because it sounds way better than acknowledging it's a nation of self-centered cretins.

So when Ken Seeroi first came to Japan, he had the genius idea of packing a suitcase full of cough syrup, pain killers, and Pepto-Bismol. Yeah, don't do that. The moment a Customs officer opens your Samsonite, the dude's gonna cream his little Japanese jeans. What's legal elsewhere is often banned here, including some prescription medications. So unless you want to spend several hours in a white room trying to translate "Flintstone's Chewables" into Japanese with your butt cheeks spread, leave that stuff at home.

Instead—and I know you probably won't do this but you really should—just check into your hotel and then head to the nearest drugstore for some ibuprofen and antacid. For about ten bucks, it's the cheapest insurance you'll ever buy. In Japanese, stomach medicine is *igusuri* (胃薬), and ibuprofen's just, well, *i-bu-pu-ro-fen* (イブプロフェン). The "i"'s are pronounced as "ee"'s, by the way. You can thank me later.

4. Illegal Drugs

I know a dude, let's just call him Jacob, since that's his name, who majored in Japanese in college, got to the point of speaking it pretty well, then interviewed and landed a job in

Tokyo. You can probably guess where this is going. After three months of teaching English, dating girls, and basically living the dream, Jacob got himself busted at a party for smoking pot. He spent a couple weeks in a Japanese jail, then got deported. His first email from the U.S. contained only one line: "I've ruined my life."

Look, it isn't easy getting to Japan. Even coming for a visit takes a nice stack of cash, and moving here is a major ordeal of securing a job, visa, and apartment. Then do one thing wrong and Boom, you're on a 737 back to Oklahoma. Japan's not cool with drugs. Me personally, I've got no beef with however you want to live your life, but know you're taking an enormous risk in using any kind of illegal drugs in Japan. And carrying them through Customs?—Man, you're on your own with that.

If you do drugs, let me tell you how you'll get busted. Think about if you were at a party with like a famous actor or basketball player or something. And then all of a sudden he fired up a crack pipe or started making out with this cross-dressing prostitute. Would you tell anyone? Hell yeah, you would! You'd be on the phone with your buddy, like, "Guess who I saw smoking crack and making out with a dude in a dress? No, not me. Someone else."

Well, that's basically you in Japan. You stand out, and no matter what you do, people are gonna talk about it. Like the Breck Syndrome, they'll tell two friends, and they'll tell two friends, until one morning a couple detectives come knocking on your door. This is true of drugs, but it's also true of other things in general. I hate to say it, but don't share secrets with Japanese people. It's not their fault. You're just too damned interesting.

5. Food

One of the main reasons I came to Japan was for the food, so whenever I travel to the U.S., I take a suitcase full of *dry natto*, *umeboshi*, and *katsuobushi*, just to confound the American Customs officers. But most people aren't me. I've learned that. So you're probably going to want to bring whatever horrible Captain Crunch or Nestle's Quick you can't live without. Bear in mind, of course, that Japan is a well-developed, international country, so you can fulfill your desire for a bag of tortilla chips bigger than your apartment and a block of cheese the size of a human head at Costco. Also, don't bring anything prohibited, like weasels. But they're for personal consumption. Yeah, right.

6. Toiletries

Japan has an astonishing array of soap, hair-, and skin-care products, so why anyone would want to bring their own is a mystery to me, but some people do. I guess if you're crazy about your Prell or Crest with Triple Whitening Action you'd better bring it, but realistically, you can probably find the same or better here.

7. The Internet

Okay, you can't really bring this, but you're gonna have to deal with it right away, so let me tell you what little I know. First of all, Japan has relatively limited free Wi-Fi. Don't expect to find a hotspot pretty much anywhere on the street. Starbucks, however, is your friend. You can also crouch in front of Family Mart with a can of *chu-hi* and download all your Netflix, if need be.

If you're moving here, you may want to consider getting a smartphone and tethering it, instead of setting up a landline at your apartment. Japan has pretty blazing fast LTE, and then you can use your PC at home, at work, in the *izakaya*, wherever. To do so, you're either going to need a Japanese smartphone, or somehow get your smartphone to work in this country, but you'd need to do that anyway. Another option is a wireless modem, like a personal hotspot. I had one for a while, and it worked great too, but now that I've got an iPhone, it does double duty as a modem as well. It's worth comparing the cost of tethering versus a landline, considering your anticipated data usage.

8. Books and Magazines

The thing about paper is, it's crazy heavy, since books are just ground up trees, so you're gonna want to think twice about bringing your leather-bound Chronicles of Narnia collection. On the other hand, the range of English-language novels and periodicals is incredibly limited in Japan, so if there's something you really want to read, maybe you should bring it or figure out how to download it to a Kindle or something.

To tell the truth, about ninety percent of what I brought to Japan ended up in the trash within a year. I packed three suits and a couple pairs of cool jeans that turned out to be way out of style, not that I had a clue at first. I just assumed Ken Seeroi was fashionable no matter what. But all of the expensive shirts and ties I brought—jeez, what was I thinking? If I had to do it again, I wouldn't spend a yen on clothing before I left; I'd just come with a pocketful of cash and an empty suitcase, then go straight to the first UNIQLO when I got off the plane. Honestly, you could probably come to Japan with no suitcases at all. Now that would be cool.

Why You Shouldn't Learn Japanese

Anyone with an interest in Japan should learn a little Japanese. I really believe that. Daily life is much better when you know a few key phrases: Hello. My name is. Please. May I? No really, please. Why not? Oh come on, please. You sure? Last chance. Well fine, be that way. Sorry for causing a scene. Even if I pay you? No? Hmph, well I didn't want to anyway.

But when I say "a little" of the language, I mean it. Beyond a handful of survival sentences, you should give a really good think as to whether or not you want to continue learning Japanese.

So someone on Facebook recently asked me: What's the best way to begin learning Japanese, for someone starting from zero? Never one to shirk his authorial duties, I did the responsible thing by jumping up, slamming my laptop closed, and running to the convenience store for a bottle of cheap white wine and a bag of spicy dried corn snacks. They're super salty, but man, are they ever good. But then at the store I ran into this girl named Misa and she invited me over for some tea, and then we drank the wine, and then a bottle of red she had, and suddenly I woke up and it was 4 a.m. and I didn't know where I was, so by the time I got home I'd forgotten all about the question. But I really meant to answer it. Sometimes Japan just gets in the way like that.

So the very first step is to find yourself a really tall mountain. The taller the better, preferably with a sturdy pine tree. Climb to the mountaintop and sit there. If there's a pine tree, then climb to the top of that and sit there instead. Then stay there for exactly one week. You should probably pack some sandwiches, now that I think about it, and definitely a cooler of beer too. Just think how refreshing that'd be. And while you're there with your pine cones and sandwiches and beer, ask yourself: Do I really want to study Japanese? No, really. Because here's what it's all about.

I want to tell the world that learning Japanese is easy and

fun. Because that'd be great and the world would like that, and then I could sell everyone some secret method I'd dreamed up and be rich and the people of all nations would be happy. But on a scale of 1 to Hot-Tub-at-the-Playboy-Mansion, learning Japanese slots in somewhere between soldering together your own black-and-white TV and copying the Bible with a quill pen while wearing a Medieval monk outfit. Plus, it takes a really long time.

Look, everyone thinks they can learn Japanese quickly, fueled in part, no doubt, by the number of books and websites claiming to help you do so if you buy their products. But frankly, when I look at the very few people I know who've actually succeeded, it's clear why. They got up at 4 a.m. every morning to do speaking drills, or wrote 50,000 flash cards, or went to language school five hours a day. Myself, I can truthfully say I've spent at least 10,000 hours actively studying, and that's not counting watching Japanese movies, singing karaoke, having conversations all day long in Japanese, and working in Japan.

Part of the problem lies with ever-loftier goals. At first, I thought it would be enough just to master some survival phrases. But every time I met someone, they asked me questions I couldn't answer. So I learned more, until I could finally have a conversation. Then I wanted to have longer, more interesting conversations, until eventually I realized what I really needed was to make myself understood in both speech and writing at roughly the same level I'm at in English. In other words, even fluency wasn't enough. It's a little bit like putting yourself through high school and college all over again, alone, in Japanese.

If I had to say how long it would take to get reasonably good at Japanese, I'd estimate a minimum of five to seven years, and possibly much more, depending upon how much time you devote and how many advantages you bring to the table.

Of the hundreds of people I've seen study Japanese over the years, only about ten succeeded in speaking the language with any level of competency. The rest eventually stopped. You might want to give some thought to undertaking a project with a higher dropout rate than that of the Navy SEALs. Just saying.

"Men wanted for hazardous journey. Low wages, bitter cold, long hours of complete darkness. Safe return doubtful. Honour and recognition in event of success."
—Sir Earnest Shackleton

Of course, you can spend the years of your life any way you like, but it seems a shame to buy a cookbook, go to the store for eggs, flour and a cake pan, come home and mix up a batter, put it in the oven, and then half an hour later yank open the oven and chuck the whole thing out the window. In other words, either bake cake or do not, there is no try. Yoda said that.

Most people seem to last about a year. At that point, Japan's still a fantasy land and they're all balls-out to learn the language. Then after several months it dawns on them that it's a much bigger task than they were led to believe. So be aware of how long it's going to take. If you want to spend the years, you absolutely can do it. Well, maybe you can. But think about whether you want to spend a couple decades on Japanese before you set out. Doing it halfway seems kind of a waste of time.

"Opportunity cost" is a term economists use to make you feel bad about your behavior. If you spent ten dollars on a delicious dinner, well, see there Ken, that's money you could've invested in the stock market, and now you'd be rich and have two delicious dinners. That kind of stuff.

Studying Japanese takes some money, but more importantly, it takes time. In the 10 to 20 years you spent learning Japanese, you could have learned to play the guitar, and now you'd be in a cool rock band and getting lots of sex. Or you could've gone to the gym and now you'd have abs of steel, and be getting lots of sex. Or gone back to college and be getting lots of sex.

Contrary to what you may think, learning Japanese will not help you have lots of sex in Japan. It'll actually retard you. Literally, you'll be a retard. Stick with English, trust me.

But let's not use the word "problem." Let's say "challenge." And one of the challenges—oh the hell with it—the *problem* with Japanese is it's pretty much only useful in Japan. So how long are you gonna be in Japan? Let's say you turn out to be some super prodigy kind of dude and learn Japanese in just two years. Great, now I hate you. Don't get uppity. If you stay in Japan for two years, then that's 1:1 and maybe it was worth the time investment. But what if it takes you five years to learn and you only stay for a year? See what I'm saying? I've known people who spent years learning Japanese and watching anime and reading manga and then once they got here, eh, it wasn't as great as they thought it'd be, and they went home. Open window, toss cake.

On top of that, you really don't need Japanese. Of the more than twenty countries I've visited, Japan's probably the most set up to accommodate people who don't speak the local language. Many foreigners live here with no more than a handful of simple phrases and do just fine. Lots of signs and menus are in English, and the entire population has received at least six years of English education. Not to mention the fact it's not an accident your local restaurant doesn't have an English menu. Everybody's got Google Translate. That's a conscious choice—they don't want a bunch of dopey *gaijin* wrecking the atmosphere.

Even if you try to speak Japanese, it may not work. Sometimes no matter how perfectly you ask a question in Japanese, you'll get an answer in English, or at least dumbed-down Japanese. Contrary to many countries that demand you speak the local language, Japan often prefers you *don't* speak Japanese.

You know David Blaine, the magician guy? Think about like him at a party. People see the dude and just wig out—Wow, David Blaine! Do some card tricks or hold your breath for ten minutes or something! And he's like, Nah, I just want to drink a beer like everybody else. That would suck, right? You'd be like, I went to a party with stupid David Blaine and he didn't even levitate or anything.

Well that's you in Japan, unless you look super Japanese, and then people will be confused until they figure out you're secretly white. Your magic trick is you can speak English. That's what everyone wants you to do. And every time you do it, and tell them about how big the cheeseburgers are back home and how people wear shoes inside the house, their eyes will light up and they'll be like, Wow, *sugoi*!

And every time you speak Japanese, people will say, "Oh, your Japanese is so good." And then try to speak English with you. You can say the most profound thing ever in Japanese, make the funniest joke, claim you invented cheese toast—and all you'll get back is "*Heeeeey*." But say any stupid thing off the top of your head in English and everybody busts up laughing. English is a pretty upbeat language; Japanese, eh, not so much. And when it comes to meeting people of the opposite sex, and potentially even having that sex, well, they don't want you to be like everybody else. They want the magic.

If you came to Japan for a vacation, you probably had a pretty mind-blowing time. Everything was new, and everything was interesting. But it was also, in a sense, free, because you used money you'd saved up or you credit-carded it or something. Either way, you didn't have to work in Japan in exchange for the experience you were having.

But once you live and work here, that changes. You can go clubbing, take trips to *onsen*, hang out all night in karaoke booths, but you have to work in order to make those things possible. And the more fun you want to have, the more you have to work. That realization changes the equation. It's not fun for free once you live here.

Now, I like Japan, don't get me wrong. And I like conversing in Japanese, and reading and writing it. But Japan's still just a place, with plenty of both good and bad. That's why it's called

Japan, and not Heaven. The architecture is—mmm, not so great. The natural scenery—yeah, that's not so great either. The people—ah jeez, well, you get the idea. But hey, at least the food's good. That's something.

So if you never wanted to learn Japanese, here's your big chance to do absolutely butt nothing. On the other hand, if you still really, really want to study Japanese, and make it a significant part of your life's work, then I'm a hundred percent behind you. Well, maybe like ninety, but that's still pretty good. So it's probably safe to come down out of that tree now and spend the rest of your days working on it. Yeah, come to think of it, maybe you better stay up there a bit longer.

Japan, After the Love

And then somehow I ended up in Fukuoka for Golden Week, eating at this *yatai* along the river. It all had something to do with a Japanese girl and way too much sake, as I recall. That is, assuming I could recall, which actually I can't. Still, Golden Week's a great holiday in Japan, since everyone has Friday and Monday off from work, and those two days magically add up to being called "a week." That's some high-level Japanese math for you. Anyway, it was golden.

Unfortunately, there's no English word for *yatai*, probably because no Westerner ever dreamed of serving steaming bowls of ramen and chicken skewers from half a shack cobbled together out of old doors and tattered shower curtains. But Fukuoka's got a string of these little rickety stalls on the banks of its black river, lit up at night with bare lightbulbs and red paper lanterns, full of wobbly drunks perched on folding chairs tossing back beer and shochu. And since the night was lovely and warm, I picked a yatai with a friendly orange sign, where customers were being welcomed with small plates of edamame and fish eggs mixed with chopped green onions. So hospitable, the Japanese.

So last week someone asked me what Japan's like "once the mystical halo around kanji characters disappears?" Ah, the halo...how I miss mine. Where'd I put that damn thing? Probably under the pile of beer cans on my balcony, along with my last paycheck, is where. But yeah, the more of the language you know, the more you understand how Japan works. That's like when Adam bit the apple. Sure, it was great because he got to eat this delicious apple and all, but also not good because, well hell, I dunno, but there was this snake and some big problem ensued, and some chick was involved too. There's always a woman in the middle of things, for some reason. Remind me to Wikipedia this.

Now looking back at when I first got to Japan, everything was fabulous, hilarious, marvelous, and if I could think of another word ending in -ous, I'd add that too. My coworkers liked me, girls wanted to date me, and people on the street couldn't wait to be my friend. I was utterly clueless and believed it all. What a great country! I took pictures of everything. Look how small my hotel room is! Look, an old Buddhist temple! Definitely getting a photo of that. Whoa, a woman in an elaborate kimono, randomly strolling the alleys of Kyoto with a red umbrella. A geisha, what incredible luck! And now I've got a photo album filled with pictures of tourists dressed up as fake geisha.

So these days, well, it's not easy to take pictures, since all the temples have become as interesting as churches and a kimono is less remarkable than a cool pair of jeans. I mean, who takes pictures of things they see every day? It's all just so insanely normal. Don't worry, I know I'm jaded, but only when sober, so you can rest easy. Doesn't happen too often.

And maybe that's the most surprising thing about Japan after all these years: just how unsurprising it really is. Once all the stuff you don't understand wears off, it's kind of, well, an average place. Not bad or anything, but not so different from anywhere else. Japanese people, for their part, try hard to boost it up, with constant reminders like, You know we eat raw fish—you subsist on hot dogs. We drink green tea—you like Coke, right? We're subtle—you're not. Yeah, about that. It's practically a Japanese hobby to convince people how different they are from you.

Kanji is the final bastion of Japanese resistance, since it's the one thing "you foreigners" are almost guaranteed not to understand. Which reminds me of when I was ten and wanted to write messages in secret code. I didn't even have anything secret to write—being ten, of course—but for some reason it seemed like the best idea ever. Until I was, uh, eleven. But sometimes it feels like Japanese people are still at it. Like, would it kill you to put some *furigana* over things? Oh right, your secret language, I forgot.

Actually, I used to take lots of pictures of Japanese signs. I was like, Who cares what they say—look at all that kanji! But now, having studied a bit of Japanese, I've been looking back at those photos. Here's a small sampling, now that I can read them:

Please don't spit your gum into the toilet.
Groping others on the train is a crime.
Let's not throw our garbage in the river.
Please don't dry your hands on the dish towel.
Beware of dark strangers approaching you at night.
Stop abandoning your pets by the reservoir.

Somehow I thought Japan was way more Zen than that, like all the signs would say something profound, or at least interesting, but mostly it's the same stuff you'd find anywhere, prohibitions and warnings, telling you not to do whatever you were just about to. Japan's a lot less Karate Kid than it seems at first. Guess you'll have to do something else with your puppy.

There's a lot of good stuff about Japan. It's generally clean, the trains run on time, and the food's fantastic. Also, you're probably not going to get shot to death, so that's a plus. Although you could get nuclear bombed by North Korea, so okay, let's just call it even. Sure, there's some stuff that's not so great, but hey that's anywhere. Well, except for Denmark. But water finds its own level. That's the right aphorism, isn't it? I'll take your silence as a yes.

So the yatai with the orange sign was going off, with people pouring in and out. That is, as much as a wooden shack can "go off" without toppling over. I watched this wrinkly old couple behind the counter shout a Japanese "Welcome!" as a businessman walked in. Then "Welcome!" they sang out as a couple walked in. A pair of girls went in, and—"Welcome!" Just my kind of spot, so in I went. The wrinkly old man looked up. The whole place fell silent. "No English menu," he said.

Bit of a rough start, but beggars can't be choosers. Nor can paying customers, apparently. "Japanese is fine," I said in Japanese. He pointed to a folding chair, and I sat down. People started talking again, a bit quieter than before.

"Beer, please," I said in Japanese, "and one of those grilled sardines stuffed with cod roe."

He stared at me. Then replied, in English, "Fish okay?"

"Uhhh, fish okay."

The wrinkly woman handed me a bottle of beer and a diminutive glass that might've been clean about a decade ago. Then this random chick to my left toasted with me, and we launched into a conversation in Japanese and I felt considerably better. Beer helps. She had on a brightly colored shawl and oversized glasses that made her face look like a squirrel. It turned out she'd just come down from Tokyo, where she worked in a boutique. "Me too," I said. I meant about Tokyo, not the boutique, and so we laughed. I'm funny like that. Then she noticed I didn't have an appetizer, so she pointed this out to the wrinkly woman. That's when I noticed all the other customers had small plates of edamame and fish eggs with green onions.

"We don't give them to foreigners," said Wrinkly Woman to Woman-like-Squirrel.

"Oh," said Squirrel.

"This happens," I explained. "Gaijin have one beer and leave. Then when they get the bill, they don't understand why they were charged for an appetizer. It's okay."

"They don't understand the system," said Wrinkles to Squirrel, without looking at me.

"That's true," I said. "The appetizer's an extra charge. But for Japanese people, well, we stay a while, so it works out fine."

"So foreigners don't get appetizers?" Asked Squirrel. She glanced at me.

"Gaijin complain about the charge," said Wrinkles.

"I'd like one," I said. "I actually like fish eggs, and edamame."

Wrinkles walked to the other end of the counter. I thought maybe she was going to get my appetizer, but it never materialized.

"I'm sorry," said Squirrel.

"It's okay" I said. "Happens all the time."

That's kind of the way it is. Nice people, and not-so-nice people. Stuff that's fun, and stuff that's not. When I first got to Japan, it felt like I'd left real life behind. But it was there all along, just below the surface. I just didn't get it. But then, I don't get a lot of things.

The Squirrel and I sat under the red paper lanterns and chatted for a couple hours, had a bunch more beer, then some sake, a few skewers of grilled shrimp and mushrooms, and then some more beer. Then some more sake, until she suddenly started to look a whole lot more attractive. I love when that happens. The night was warm and mellow. More customers came in, were welcomed, got appetizers, and pretty soon we were all drinking together, almost as though I fit in.

Renewing a Japanese Visa, More Fun Every Year

Ah, May. What a wonderful month. The seasonal rains wash away winter, it's finally warm enough to sleep without a fur hat, and I get to enjoy renewing my Japanese visa. That's how I know spring has come.

Unfortunately, unlike going to the Japanese doctor, or getting arrested by the Japanese police, there's no apparent redeeming quality to visiting the Immigration Bureau. It's crowded, you have to line up for hours, and unlike the rest of Japan which is full of nice, clean Japanese people, it's packed full of foreigners. Eeeew.

Exactly a year ago, in May, I went through the same process. At that time, when I got the visa renewal paperwork from my supervisor, I noticed something concerning.

"I'm looking at this 'Period of Work' field," I said gently. My supervisor's a Japanese woman, so I try to be a little more charming, by using my bedroom voice.

"Yes?" she said.

"You see, it seems you wrote a '1' here," I said huskily, "which means a one-year visa, and I'd have to go back again next year." I tried to smile.

"Yes, that's...correct," she said.

"The thing is," I said, gazing into her eyes, "you could write anything, you know. Like, say a '3' or a '5.' Five's a nice number, pleasingly symmetrical, don't you think?"

"Sorry, but your contract says one year," she said, and tried to smile.

"I, uh, don't actually have a contract," I said, smiling back. "Just a job description, in English. There's nothing signed. And really, every other company writes a '3.'"

"I'll have to check with HR," she said.

"*Yoroshiku onegaishimasu,*" we both said. That's Japanese for, "Please don't screw this up." But it sounds polite, so that makes it okay.

But right then, I knew it was over. Check with HR? You might as well check with Jesus. And sure enough, I only got a 1-year extension, which is nothing, since a year in Japan passes with the speed of a month in the U.S. To prove this, I hung out my bath towel this morning, and it was dry in 30 minutes. Explain that.

And so now, a year later, here we are, again the same conversation. And again, she writes a "1." And we smile at each other. Bitch.

Now, the thing about Ken Seeroi is, nothing phases him. Like I could be on a golf course in the middle of a thunderstorm with lightning all around, and I'd be holding a one iron like, Where's everybody running off to? Like freaking Ahab on deck in a typhoon in Moby Dick, with a harpoon or something. Just brandishing the thing. Assuming I golfed, of course. You'd look at me and be like, Ken Seeroi, you my friend, have nerves of steel. You should've been a brain surgeon, or an army sniper, or a whaler, or at least on the PGA Tour, instead of an English teacher. And while I'd appreciate your saying so, I'd know that really, inside, I'm actually not so cool with lots of stuff. My nerves are more like gummi bears, or I dunno, some other soft object. Like when people call me a *gaijin* or *gaikokujin*. See now, that bothers me. I don't know why, exactly. Hand me the English menu. Oooh, that really bothers me. Renew my visa for 1 year? Are you fucking kidding? Just write down a damned "3" for Godsakes. If I had a pen, I would have stabbed her through the heart. But because I'm so cool, I just grinned and said, "Thank you." Grrrr. I really gotta remember my pen.

This threw me into a tailspin. The whole visa process seems designed to reinforce the message—You don't actually live here, remember? Like the difference between a jazz bar, and your house. You get all comfy on the sofa with some mellow music, a gin and tonic, maybe some peanut snacks, until suddenly the lights come on and a big guy makes you leave. That's not okay. Why is there a large man in my house? I started to consider my options. If I have to do this every year, I thought, Screw it, maybe I'll just go back to America.

Back in the U.S. of A. No more being stared at, no more salarymen clamoring to speak to the white guy. Nobody telling me how well I use a fork. America. That'd solve everything. Except for the fact I'd have to live with a bunch of *gaijin*. Okay, so that's kind of a drawback. And the food, ah, jeez. What would I subsist on without fried octopus balls and okra with fish flakes? A diet of corn dogs and Pop Tarts? Nah, fuck that, I thought, I'll get married. Visa? Fixed. Instant family and social circles? Done. Get an apartment, car, and somebody to read all the stuff in my mailbox. A wife. That'd solve everything. Well, except for the part where I'd have a wife. Ah, maybe I could sort that out later. Jeez, there's always some little detail that complicates my genius plan.

So this year, again, when I filled in my portion of the visa renewal form, I wrote a "5" in the field for "Desired length of extension." And again, I refrained from writing "inches" after the "5," which I felt showed great restraint and maturity. Not that the Immigration Bureau noticed last year, seeing as they gave me a disappointing 1-year extension. Sure, one extra is better than nothing, but five's what I really wanted. Heh, a total of 17 inches. Now that would be awesome.

Sorry. I'm so juvenile. Back on track. So this year, again with the whole visa thing. I went to the Immigration Bureau, which took hours, because I had to ride the train, then ride the bus, and then walk. Very tiring, all that using of the legs and such. And on top of everything, the renewal cost 40 bucks, only in yen. That's like 4,000 yens, which sounds even more expensive. Then when I handed in the form, the Immigration lady said in Japanese, "Oh, you need some other documents."

"Other documents?" I said. Whenever I don't know what to say in Japanese, I just repeat the other person's last words.

"Yes, you need to go to City Hall and get this tax information." She handed me the world's longest and most complicated Japanese tax form ever. It was like a haiku crossword puzzle.

"This tax information?" I said. "You do realize I can read exactly none of what you just handed me."

"Then mail it back to us in this envelope."

"So I need to go to City Hall, get some documents I don't understand, and mail them to you in this envelope?"

"That's it," she said.

"Don't suppose you could just call City Hall and have 'em faxed? My visa expires this Friday, you know." I was pretty stressed at this point, because I'd, uh, kind of put off the whole visa thing for about a month too long. I guess that was kind of my fault.

"Just mail everything when you can," she said. "No rush."

I stared at her. No rush? This is the country where the entire subway platform commits ritual *seppuku* if the train's thirty seconds late. Since when did Japan turn into Jamaica? No rush? Nobody in the history of this nation's ever uttered that phrase. People here get jailed and deported for overstaying their visas. "Oh, I can do that," I said. "No rush happens to be my best thing," and walked away trying to focus my eyes on the tax form.

I went home and spent a few days deciphering what documents I needed, all the while hearing her words, which seemed to acquire more of a Jamaican accent as time went by, like "No rush, mon." Then it took me almost a week to make it to City Hall, and by then I was officially overstaying my Japanese visa big time. I tried to picture what I'd say when the police showed up at my door. "Yah but da Immigration Lady she say it be no rush, one love." They'd never buy that. Then right on cue, a couple days after I'd mailed the documents, my doorbell rang. Holy God, nobody ever rings my doorbell. I stayed absolutely still. Actually it was pretty easy since I was laying on the floor drinking beer and watching YouTube clips about army snipers. Man, do those guys have nerves of steel. I paused the video and waited a few minutes before I felt the coast was clear. Then I belly-crawled to the fridge and got another beer.

Due to Golden Week, it took almost two more weeks before a postcard came in the mail from the Immigration Bureau.

I knew this meant one of two possible things. One would be that I'd get a 1-year visa extension. The other would be that it was a sting operation to catch foreigners who'd overstayed their Japanese visas. I stuffed a change of socks and underwear into my bag, just in case. Ken Seeroi knows what's up. Gotta be prepared.

So before I left, I stopped at Starbucks to say goodbye to everyone, then went to my neighborhood shrine, to ask Japanese God to watch over my aunt who is recovering from heart surgery, plus my Japanese friend with cancer. And my American friend with cancer. And my American cat with cancer. Jeez, Japanese God's gonna be mighty busy. Hope he's got a sled like Santa or something to help him get around. And although it seemed petty and self-serving by comparison, I asked Him for a visa extension. Since I was there and all, I figured why not sneak it in.

Then I rode the train. And I rode the bus. And I waited in line until they called my number and then handed the Immigration lady the postcard, and waited some more. I took a little nap. Then they called my number again and I went sleepily back to the window.

The Immigration lady handed me back my passport and my old residence card, with a hole punched through it. Then she gave me a new card, with baby blue stripes. Centered on top, in small letters, it said "Residence Card," which seemed kind of redundant, and down below, next to "Period of Stay," the number three. She smiled. I couldn't believe it. The U.S. President only gets four years, and he's the leader of the free world. I smiled back. The card had a shining Ministry of Justice hologram, practically radiating hope. The Ministry of Freaking Justice loved me, and had independently and mysteriously decided to award me three more years in their special nation. It was the most beautiful card I'd ever seen.

I bounded outside like sunbeams were lighting my way. Which was a good thing, because actually the sky was a sheet of gray and everybody was shuffling around staring at their phones. But ah, springtime in Japan, and I wasn't in prison. It was lovely. I went straight to Starbucks, where it's always sunny, and the staff and customers crowded around and agreed how beautiful my new residence card was. Then back to the shrine, where I realized everything was again right in the world. Well, at least for three more years. Thanks a bunch, Japanese God.

The Japanese Festival I Never Saw

I love Skype, if only because my brother can drunk-dial me from the U.S., where it's apparently nighttime, even it's 5 a.m. in Japan and I'm fast asleep in my futon.

I answered in the customary fashion.

"Yo, nigga."

"My nigga!" he bellowed. This is how white people talk when black people aren't around. "Wha's happenin'?"

"I'm dreaming I'm still asleep is what," I mumbled. "I gotta go to some festival with this Japanese chick today."

"Cool, what's the festival?"

"Like what do you mean?"

"Like, is it celebrating an event or something?"

"Man, I dunno," I said. "There's freaking festivals here all the time. Maybe it's for summer, or"—and suddenly I remembered how cheap tomatoes have been for some reason. My mind's strange like that. But four for a dollar? Such a deal— "the tomato harvest or something."

"Well, have a good time at your tomato festival," he said. "I'm gonna go drink a beer."

"Yeah, you do that," I said.

And then I couldn't go back to sleep. So I got up and ate a pack of *natto*. I don't know why more people don't like natto. It's just beans. What kind of Grinch doesn't like beans? Plus it's cheap as all hell, and you can scarf a whole pack in like ten seconds. That's time efficiency. Sure, it makes your breath smell like poo and is sticky as hell if you get it on your face, but just eat carefully. Avoid your face. And brush your teeth like twice. Anyway, it's a good breakfast, is what I'm trying to say.

The truth is, I've been on a diet lately. I call it the Natto Diet. That's where you eat a pack of natto for breakfast, and then, well, just try not to eat anything else for as long as you can possibly stand it. Not really much of a plan, I guess. Okay, so I'm still working out the kinks.

So then about noon, my friend Hina called to tell me we'd have to ride the train way out to the countryside to get to the festival.

"Ken, are you ready?" she asked. "Because we have to ride the train way out to the countryside."

"Why?" I asked.

"To get to the festival," she said.

"I see," I said. "Give me a couple minutes. I gotta brush my teeth again. Meet you at the station."

Part of working out the kinks includes running to the station and giving up drinking. Now, I know what you're thinking. Ken Seeroi give up drinking? That's impossible. Ah, so you'd think—but you don't know about my amazing willpower. It's...well, amazing. I hadn't had a drink in three days, which I believe is some kind of world record. And running to the station—well, actually I was just late. But it still counts as exercise.

Hina was dressed in pink platform shoes, tight jeans, and a pink blouse. I think her purse matched her belt too, but maybe I just dreamed that. She had long hair and fake eyelashes. That kind of Japanese girl, if that makes any sense. But she doesn't speak English, so I like her.

"I'm hungry," she said in pouty Japanese. "Let's get a rice ball and some snacks for the train."

"You go ahead," I said. "I'm on a diet. The Natto Diet."

"What's that?"

"I'll explain on the way."

And so we rode the train and she ate her rice ball and then some of these rice crackery things with peanuts and I sat there and got hungrier and hungrier. It was almost two p.m. But I didn't give in. That's the power of the natto diet. It only makes you think you're going to die.

So we got to the festival and there was music and children laughing and all these Japanese guys carrying around giant wooden shrines and yelling, but all I could think about was food. Food, everywhere I looked were food stalls. With food.

Amazing scents were wafting from every direction. Fried pancakes. Fried noodles. Fried octopus balls. French fries. Okay, so there was a lot of fried stuff. But no tomatoes, strangely. Still, once Ken Seeroi decides he's on a diet, he sticks with it.

"Ken!" said Hina. "Look, buttered potatoes!"

I tried not to look. Festival buttered potatoes are to Ken Seeroi what—what's that stuff that kills Superman? Kryptonite? Yeah, that's it. Does he like to eat it? No? Well, so much for that analogy. I took one glance at the bright sign featuring a huge baked potato covered in corn and completely lost my mind.

I ran right up to the booth, where a giant, buttery man was standing. He looked delicious.

"One please," I said in Japanese.

He pulled a giant baked potato out of a steaming wooden box and looked at me. Then he looked at Hina like he was trying to solve some sort of equation. "Does he want butter?" he asked her. This happens sometimes, on account of my whiteness.

"Yes, he does," I said.

The potato-man plunged a metal spatula into a plastic tub and what emerged was a scoop of margarine the size of a small child. He looked at Hina again. "Does he want corn?" he asked.

"Yes, he does," I said again.

At which point he made my potato disappear under an avalanche of corn and margarine. It was magical. Well, I figured, that pretty much guarantees my ass is gonna be the size of a Buick, but I mean, really, what can you say? Ya want butter? Ya got butter. Then we played the game some more. Does he want salt? How about pepper? Cheese powder? You know, if you've never really thought about all the stuff you could put on a potato, there's a surprising lot. At this point, I figured Ah, the hell with it and told him Yes, he wants *it all*. Everything. What else ya got? Mayonnaise? Bring it. Cayenne pepper? Do that shit. In the end I got the world's biggest potato floating in a sauce of seasoned butter and niblets with the caloric potential to feed a small village. Gotta say though, man, it tasted pretty fantastic.

Well, so much for that diet, I figured. But at least I hadn't had any beer, so that was a good thing. I was proud of myself, actually, and my amazing willpower.

"Let's get a beer," Hina chirped.

"Okay," I replied. I suddenly realized I was thirsty as hell. Probably shouldn't have had all that salty stuff, come to think of it.

So we had a couple tall beers and they were delicious. Then we ran into some of Hina's friends. They all had long hair, platform shoes, and pink shirts. And fake eyelashes. And they all crowded around me.

"Oooh! Take my picture with Ken!"

"Me too! Oooh, let's all take a picture with Ken together."

I was immediately engulfed in Japanese women. Now, I like that, what with the breasts and the high voices and the smelling nice and all, but I used to think they liked me because I was charming and good-looking. Now I know they just crave attention, from anyone. Still, they're cute in their neediness. Like kittens. Kittens who are freaking attention whores. But still, you gotta appreciate the warm and cuddly factor.

Then someone suggested we get some beer and chocolate-covered bananas, which was the most unlikely winningest combination ever, and made me glad I'd thought of it, then some wine and these pancake things wrapped around chopsticks, then another round of beers, and then somehow we all ended up in this dimly-lit storefront on a couch with two girls' heads on my lap and I was drinking *sake* from a plastic cup. Man, you gotta love Japanese festivals. Of course, we couldn't actually see the festival from where we were sitting, but well, you seen one festival, you...eh, they're pretty much all the same, right? Plus we could hear some drumming and chanting and stuff, so that was pretty good.

But then I had to pee. Suddenly I wished I hadn't had all that beer. Gotta stick to wine. So I got up and went to find a bathroom or a tree by the river or something and this girl named Ami went with me. We wandered around the town for a bit until we found a hostess club. It was closed, but a bunch of folks were gathered in front, and agreed we could use the bathroom.

A hostess club is one of those places where you pay forty dollars an hour and a pretty girl with fake eyelashes and long hair sits with you and pours you cheap booze and rests her hand on your thigh. After I used the bathroom, I sat on the sofa and waited for Ami. Even during the day, the place felt salacious, with its black vinyl couches and oblique lighting. Suddenly Ami appeared and sat down next to me.

"Here, let's look at pictures," she said, and took a camera from her purse, which I noticed matched her belt. We started looking at pictures. She put her hand on my thigh.

I looked at her. "Your eyes are so blue," I said.

"Yours are so brown."

"Color contacts, huh?"

"Your girlfriend would probably be mad if she saw us like this," she giggled.

"See, I find the term 'girlfriend' to be really ambiguous...you know...sure, 'friend,' and 'girl' of course, but that doesn't really mean..."

And then suddenly one of the guys from the hostess club came in. He looked at me, then at Ami, then back at me. I guess we'd been in there for like ten minutes after all. We stood up, and Ami apologized, and we all looked uncomfortably at each other for a moment, and then we left.

Ami and I went back to the storefront and Hina handed me a glass of wine. "I was worried about you two," she said.

"Jeez, we were only gone a couple minutes," I said. "Here, I, uh, bought you an ice cream."

"It was half an hour."

"Time flies, you know. Sorry, I took a few bites already."

"Thanks, I love vanilla. You didn't get one?"

"Mine? Oh, I'm on a diet, remember?"

And then we all sat on the couch and someone brought out a bottle of *shochu* and ice, and then some *oden* appeared, with fried tofu and sliced daikon radish and hard-boiled eggs until it got dark and everyone started passing out left and right, on the couch, the folding tables, the steps to the post office. Then Hina and I had to leave, partly because it was late, and partly because I kept passing out everywhere. Then all the girls hugged me again and took more pictures. By the time we got to the station all that remained of the festival was an enormous trash pile of chopsticks and paper bowls, and two old guys in costumes asleep on the grass.

I lasted about a minute on the train before I crashed out with my face pressed to the window, and slept all the way back into the city. That's the great thing about traveling with a Japanese girl. They always wake you up when you get to your stop. So helpful, really. Always take one with you, is my advice. But since it was Sunday and there's no such thing in Japan as calling in sick on Monday, I hugged Hina goodnight and went home, where I pulled out my futon and drunk-Skyped my brother.

"You know it's five a.m. here, right?" he said.

"That's okay, I don't mind. I just called to tell you about my new diet."

"Is it one of the one's where you give up drinking?"

"No, this one's different," I said. "It's called the Festival Diet. Nothing but fried foods and booze."

"Nigga, you crazy."

"Yeah...I know," I said, as I drifted off to sleep on a raft of baked potatoes floating on a river of butter, winding its way through mountains of corn. And I dreamt of a land filled with pretty girls in platform shoes, with belts that matched their bags.

The 4 Big Japanese Beach Essentials

Summer's a wonderful season in Japan. It's finally warm enough to peel off the down parkas and ski gloves, relax in the park drinking beer, and watch the girls walk by in short skirts. Actually, they wear those in winter too. Greatest country ever, in that at least. Probably sucks to be a girl here though, having to walk by the park all winter long being ogled by some white dude in a parka drinking beer with ski gloves. If anybody asked, I figured I'd say I was a member of the ski patrol, although sadly no one ever did.

Anyway, when summer comes, I start thinking beach. Sand. Waves. Sea shells. Girls in even less clothing. You pretty much can't go wrong, and it all starts with proper preparation. Now I know what you're thinking: Should I pack some sandwiches and beer? How about a big tent and a giant umbrella? Perhaps a watermelon so I can split it like they do in Japanese movies? The answer is No, you should not, because there's only four things you really need for a trip to the beach.

The Japanese Beach Checklist

In preparation for your sandy adventure, you will need the following:

1. A stylish and well-fitting bathing suit
2. A small stack of folding cash
3. One giant can of Nair, and
4. A gastric bypass operation

Guess I should've told you this back in November. Yeah, sorry about that. Well, tape it to your fridge till next year. Ken Seeroi, thinking proactively since tomorrow.

The thing to know about the beach in Japan is that it's basically a social experiment in self-selection. That's a nice way of saying that fat people don't go there. Nor do old people, or hairy people. I realized this, oh, about one second after I arrived. So maybe I felt a little out of place. Plus, for some reason, no one was wearing sunglasses, other than me.

"We don't have to," said this girl named Naoko, "because our eyes are strong."

"My eyes are strong too," I said. I don't know why I say stupid stuff like this. It just comes out.

"But our eyes are stronger," she said. That is so her.

Strong eyes, the hell, nobody gets the better of Ken Seeroi. I took off the sunglasses. That is so me. I had to admit, though, it was pretty freaking hard to see.

But let's back up a minute and talk about getting to the beach, because one key feature of "beach" is that it's not "city." Otherwise it would be called something else entirely. Like maybe "harbor" or "seaport." What am I, a sailor? Please. What I mean is it's really freaking far away, so you'll need to ride the train with that girl named Naoko for about an hour, and she'll insist upon bringing sandwiches and beer, a tent and camping supplies better suited to Mount Everest, plus a watermelon. Know how hard it is to carry a watermelon on the train? Of course you don't. That's because no sane person ever dreamed of bringing a giant piece of fruit to a place all filled with sand.

And once you finally arrive at the train station for the beach, you're still going to have to walk about two kilometers to get to the ocean. That's like five miles. And who's going to lug the cooler, tents, ice axes, and watermelon? Not Naoko, that's for sure. There's only one thing a Japanese girl can do when faced with a walk to the beach. She will feel compelled to say the word *atsui*. That means "hot," as in "It's so hot," and "Why's it so hot?" and "My head feels like it's about to explode." Japanese words are very versatile like that.

Try saying it. *Atsui*. Now with about seventy percent more whiney voice. *Atsuuuiii*. That's better. Now walk ten feet and say it again. *Atsuuuiii*. Now make a face that says Ken, I'm dying of heatstroke and in need of medical attention, are we there yet? *Atsuuuiii*. Continue in this manner, because interestingly, there's no limit to the number of times one can say the exact same word over and over.

Now, I'd like to suggest you do not point out to Naoko that

the reason one goes to the beach is precisely because the weather's sunny. Don't say, Well, nice day for a stroll, huh? Nor should you mention that you are, in effect, acting as her personal Sherpa. Such statements will only result in Naoko becoming sullen, walking even slower, and turning your trip to the beach into a hellish *atsui* death march. Trust me. I do these things so you don't have to.

When we finally did arrive at the water's edge, at least my arms were all pumped from carrying the hundreds of pounds of gear, so I felt good enough to take off my shirt. But once I did I suddenly realized the likelihood of being shot with a tranquilizer dart and dragged off to Ueno Zoo.

A guy about 14 years old walked by, looked at me, and in Japanese mumbled, "Chest hair."

I spun around and yelled after him, "You want hair? Well, check out deez nuts."

It wasn't great, but at least it was quick. That's something.

About that time, I noticed that everyone—guys, girls, the whole freaking lot of them—was tanned, skinny, and seemed to be about fourteen. That is, from what I could tell, since all I could see were ghostly silhouettes without any sunglasses. But I figured maybe all the squinting would make my eyes look more Japanese, which would be good. At any rate, I put my shirt back on, because it was kind of chilly, what with the sea breeze and all.

The Japanese beach is actually, well, not that great. The water's gray and the sand's littered with random bits of plastic and suspicious-looking styrofoam. Plus, there's a shit-ton of people. That's a technical term. Now, I know you're going to say, Yeah sure Ken, but I bet you'd like it just fine if you weren't wearing a fur suit and had gone on a diet back in November like I told you to. To which I can only reply, Jeez, why must you say such hurtful things, Naoko? It's bad enough I've gone sun-blind already. Next time remind me to bring my man-parasol.

But the good news is that the Japanese in their wisdom have

improved upon nature with their amazing technology, and nailed together huge plywood shacks on the sand that overlook the ocean. These beach barns offer all manner of food, beer, and shelter, completely obviating the need to have carried a damn thing. This is another matter you should not bring up with Naoko, despite the fact she freaking knew it because she came to the exact same beach last year with some other poor slob. Some things you just have to let go.

Once safely out of the blinding sun, I realized we'd found the best feature of the beach, in that our shack was essentially a giant, tatami-floored *izakaya* facing the ocean. I finally understood what people mean when they talk about the serenity of the sea. We got our own 3-inch tall table and ordered cold beers and something infinitely more appealing than the loaf of soggy tuna-fish sandwiches I'd packed. Who would have thought of serving steaming hot curry at the beach? Those wacky Japanese folks, that's who, and it was freaking perfect after all that schlepping of the gear. The only remaining problem was the accursed watermelon, which I had no intention of lugging all the way back home.

"Have some watermelon?" I asked gently.

"I can't," said Naoko.

"It'll help you feel less *atsui*..."

"No, I'm too full," she said, but with 70 percent more whiny voice.

"Well, why'd you eat so much freaking curry?"

"Because it was delicious."

It's kind of hard to argue with that logic, especially since it actually was and all. Still, it left me with the dilemma. Nonetheless, I was determined to dispatch the green bowling ball to Fruit Hell once and for all. I grabbed a knife. We'd actually brought an 8-inch chef's knife to the beach, just to kill the watermelon, and I had every intention of using it.

I dragged the watermelon kicking and screaming over the sand, threw it down on a blue plastic sheet, lifted the knife above my head, and came down with a tremendous Whack!

Seeds and red fruit went everywhere as it cleaved cleanly down the middle. Watermelon juice poured over the blue sheet. I was actually kind of impressed at how good a job I did. Walk softly and carry a giant knife, that's my new motto. Actually, if you've got the knife, I guess you can walk however you like. But that's more of an American motto, I think.

We spent the rest of the day in the shack, with occasional forays down to the cold, dark water just to confirm we still weren't drunk enough to dive in. So we focused on the other traditional Japanese marine sports, namely drinking a pile of beer, taking naps, eating soggy sandwiches, and powering down as much watermelon as possible. Yeah, the ocean in Japan is awesome, from the appropriate distance. Then when the sun started sinking, we grabbed a taxi back to the station, because really, that's the only intelligent way to get to and from the beach.

Why all the White People in Japan?

I interviewed to teach English in Japan in a sunny office building in downtown Los Angeles, naively believing Japan needed a person with my unique skill set and stunning good looks. But then I'm the kind of dude who watches late-night infomercials and buys a Ginsu knife set. Actually, they work pretty well, and for $19.99, how can you go wrong? I'm a sucker for a bargain. And sitting in that conference room, drinking green tea and listening to the recruiter explain the job, I assumed that Japan didn't have enough English teachers. Turns out I was wrong.

Just as well, since I find being right all the time to be interminably boring. I like to mix things up once in a while, just to keep life interesting.

Perhaps it was my oversized American suit or freshly-minted TESL certificate, but somehow I fooled the company into believing I was a person of character and responsibility, and they sent my ass to Japan to teach in an *eikaiwa*. And I'd been here for almost six months before a coworker told me the real deal.

I was secretly hoping to sleep with her, so I'd invited her to this postwar-era restaurant and ordered beer aplenty, along with grilled shiitake mushrooms and deep-fried skewers of octopus. That tastes way better than it sounds, since Japan does this thing with batter that's akin to witchcraft. Really locks in the juices, no lie.

"You guys have it great, you know," she said.

"Howzzat?" I replied, with half an octopus hanging out of my mouth.

"Your apartment's subsidized, right? And furnished?"

"Yeah sure," I said. "Yours isn't?"

"Uh-uh, and I don't make half of what you do," she answered, and downed the remainder of her beer in an enormous gulp.

"That's crazy," I noted, and proceeded to order a couple

glasses of white wine. The plan was proceeding quite well, I must say.

In our *eikaiwa*, four of the teachers were—ah, how to explain this?—I guess you'd call them "foreign." And eight others were "Japanese." That seems like a pretty clear distinction, but really it's not, since two of the "Japanese" English teachers had been raised in the U.S., including my date for the evening, one of the "foreign" teachers had been in Japan for half his life, and another "foreigner" was American-Japanese.

"So wait," I said, with a mouthful of mushrooms and wine, "you make less, why? We do the same job." I like Japan because you can talk with your mouth full.

"Because I'm Japanese," she said.

"I thought you grew up in Hawaii?" I said. "You're as American as me."

"I lived there till I was sixteen," she said, "but we moved back to Japan."

"So that means you have to buy your own furniture? Why do you make less?"

"Wrong color passport," she said. This seemed to bum her out, and I decided to pursue a different line of conversation: Western movies. Always a good tack. How 'bout that Tom Cruise, eh? Didn't rescue the situation though, I'm sorry to report. Must've been all the wine. Mission impossible. Gotta stick with beer.

But where was I? Oh yeah, English teachers. The truth is, even way out in the Japanese boonies, you can't swing a *tanuki* without knocking a couple over. Their herds roam the nation in frightening abundance, multiplying every year. They just happen to be Japanese. So one of Japan's enduring mysteries is, why bother importing foreign English teachers if Japanese folks can already do the job for less money? Let me just take a moment to personally thank whoever brainwashed the nation of Japan into believing the following three lies:

1. Foreigners know English better

2. Foreigners have a better accent

3. Foreigners have interesting cultural knowledge

Actually, nobody believes number one, since all Japanese English teachers study grammar and pass rigorous certification tests that would fry a native speaker. My own grammar knowledge is limited to vague memories of sleeping through 9th grade English and what I picked up watching "Conjunction Junction." Like the other day I was teaching at a Junior High, and the Japanese English teacher suddenly turns to me in the middle of class and asks, "Is 'danger' a noun?"

I was like, What the eff? "Danger?" A noun? What the hell's a noun? All the kids are staring at me and I'm going, person-place-or-thing...person-place-or-thing...

"It's more of like a concept," I said. Whew, that was a close one.

Then there's the pronunciation thing. Now maybe in some Oz-like world all Japanese people speak with Charlie Chan accents and foreigners sound like they were raised in the Kansas cornfields, but the reality's way different. Quite a few Japanese English teachers have great pronunciation, even ones who've never lived abroad. Guess they watch a lot of "Sex and the City." And the foreigners...well, I've met "native English speakers" from India, the Philippines, China, the Ukraine, Texas, all kinds of places with wacky accents. Ever heard a British guy? I don't know what language that is, but blimey, it sounds bloody awful. Those folks seriously need to enroll in an American study-abroad program.

The fact is, you can be from damn near anywhere and make good money as a "native English teacher," so long as you're not from Japan.

Which brings us to number 3, "Your culture," also known as "Cool, a white guy." Nowhere is this clearer than in the elementary school system.

So after my stint at the *eikaiwa* and half a dozen other gigs, I started teaching in the public school system, where, throughout Japan, thousands of foreign English teachers

(ALTs and JETs) instruct complicated topics such as Fruits and Vegetables, Days of the Week, Zoo Animals, and Head, Shoulders, Knees, and Toes. And alongside them, Japanese English teachers, teaching the exact same thing for far less money. The English ability required to do such a job is virtually zero, which begs the question: Yo, why all the white people?

Not that I'm complaining, since it gives me a job with plenty of time to perfect my Japanese. Like last week, I worked at a grade school. Outside it was pouring rain, and I was walking down the school corridor with the Japanese English teacher, Ms. Kuroda. The windows were foggy with condensation.

"Sure is raining," she said in English.

"It's our monsoon season," I said in Japanese, which I like to do just to keep her on her toes, "but our crops need it, so that's good."

Then we passed a group of students. They all bowed and said "*konnichiwa*" to Kuroda Sensei, then started waving madly at me and shouting "hello!"

"Do you ever think it's strange that they don't say 'hello' to you?" I asked.

"What d'ya mean?" she asked.

"Since you're an English teacher and all."

"Well," she said, "I'm Japanese."

Hmmm, I thought.

"Hmmm," I said.

All Japanese children learn through the school system that when they see an Asian face, they should use Japanese. And when they see my white face, they're supposed to speak English. That's just common sense. While "Japanese" English teachers can use Japanese, Rule #1 for "foreign" teachers is "No speaking Japanese." After all, start doing that and somebody's likely to mistake you for a regular person, which is crazy. Then it's just a slippery slope towards equality, and nobody wants that.

Of course, children learn a lot of other good things at school too, like it's okay to flash-mob your foreign teacher and ride him like the pony he is. They reach out to feel my hairy arms during class, unexpectedly grab my junk, and stick their fingers in my butt. They respect me so much, they can barely contain themselves. At the end of the class, they line up to give me high fives.

"Yeah, I don't do that," I say. No way Ken Seeroi's coming in physical contact with four hundred children a day. Eighty percent have snot on their hands, and the remainder have my butt on their fingers. I'd be dead of the plague within a month.

"Why not, Ken?" asked this little boy named Mr. Maeda.

"It's Seeroi-Sensei, remember?" I said.

"Kevin-Sensei always gives us high fives," said a small girl named Ms. Iwata.

"Yeah, I don't know who that is," I said, "but do you high-five Ms. Kuroda?"

"No," they laughed, "She's Japanese."

It took me a while to figure it out, but it finally dawned on me why white people have been brought to Japan. Kuroda-Sensei helped me understand it.

"Just play some games," she said. "The kids just want to have fun with Ken-Sensei."

"Yeah, I know I'm fun and magical and all, but I don't suppose I could just teach English?"

"They really want to hear some funny stories about your culture," said Ms. Kuroda.

"Well, last time I told them Americans all ride zebras and wear meat hats. So are you telling them about the years you spent herding kangaroos in Australia, or just doing a regular English class?"

"Just a regular class. But...we're different, you and me."

"I know, you eat Western foods and your English is better. But we teach the same thing and we both live in Japan. So what's the difference?"

"Well, you know," she said, "you've got different...blood."

Ah, check and mate. There's no arguing with science. So the

truth is nobody actually flew me to Japan to teach Seasons of the Year or how to pronounce "bloccori." They just wanted the chance to touch the hairy arms of a real, live foreigner, to see how high his nose was, and marvel at his use of chopsticks. I guess if that's "cultural exchange," then hey, I'm cool with it. It's like busing, only for teachers, not students. And without it, there'd be a few thousand white, black, and miscellaneous Asian "English teachers" out of a job.

At the same time, it seems a little uninspired to prime children to look for differences rather than commonalities. By the time they leave elementary school, the kids have all read textbooks showing that French people wear berets and Africans greet each other with "Jambo." School's prepared them to say "hello" when they meet white people, serve them coffee instead of tea, and hand them the English menu. They're a different race, so why would you treat them the same? Stop with that crazy talk, already.

So after I finished a class in which I told everyone that Americans fly to work using umbrellas constructed of one hundred hot dogs, the Principal asked me to eat lunch with the kids. "They're excited to learn more about your culture," he explained. Ms. Kuroda stayed and ate in the staff room. Then while the kids and I were eating our bean stew and I was telling them all about how I invented the Beer Helmet and Giant Foam Finger, little Mr. Maeda tugged on my arm hair and whispered in sad Japanese, "Will you go home today, Ken?"

"Of course I'll go home," I said. And then little Mr. Maeda started crying.

"Whoa, easy with the waterworks," I said. "Hey there, it's okay, Seeroi-Sensei will be back tomorrow."

"But I don't know him, and you're going to America," he sobbed.

"No, silly," I said, "I live in Japan."

And then little Mr. Maeda looked very confused and even sadder, as though I'd just told him Santa was merely some dude in a red suit. "Japan?" he said, and kept on crying, while outside it looked as though the rain would never end. Sure enough, going home in the middle of that monsoon was gonna be gnarly. I was glad I didn't have to ride my zebra all the way to America, though I sure wished I'd remembered my meat hat and hundred-hot dog umbrella.

One Thing You Must Never Do in Japan

Fruit flies. I woke up and all I could see were fruit flies, which for some reason, eh, didn't seem all that unusual. Probably because when you live in Japan, strange stuff just *happens*. I don't know why. Like the other day I rolled over to find my futon soaked with sweat and the apartment about 140 degrees, despite having cranked on the A/C the night before. Hey, is it my fault "heater" and "cooler" share the same *kanji*? That's more of a product-safety issue for the thermostat manufacturer, I think. A lesser individual might've perished in his sleep. Good thing I was well hydrated with malt liquor before turning on the heater and going to bed.

All that hotness really seemed to explode the ol' fruit fly population, adding to an ever-lengthening list of stuff one shouldn't do in Japan: Don't press buttons you don't fully understand. Don't go outside without a shirt on. Don't wear shoes inside the house. Instead, wear these tiny slippers. But not on the carpet—that's only for socks. And don't wear them into the bathroom; instead, wear these other tiny slippers. See how they're different? No? Well, they are. Stepping out on the balcony without a shirt? What are you, a Neanderthal? Put on a robe and the balcony slippers, for Chrissakes.

Honestly, the county's laid with traps from floor to ceiling. Like, last weekend's a good example, since I was at this Japanese girl's apartment, and we were savoring a bottle of sweet white wine and a can of Pringles. Hey, Ken Seeroi's the kind of guest who doesn't show up empty-handed. I mean, like thoughtful, because who doesn't enjoy the subtle flavors of sour cream and onion? Please. And she had this lovely glass lamp hanging from the ceiling in the middle of her place. It was beautiful. You can probably see where this is going. So when I walked in, the very first thing she said, even before Hello, was, Don't hit your head. Yeah, well, that lasted about a minute. Can I help it if I'm descended from a race of people with amazingly durable skulls? That's actually a genetic advantage. Google it. Anyway, you'd be surprised how much glass one small lamp's capable of producing, as were we. I was just glad I'd put the lid back on the Pringles. Safety first, I always say.

My point—if I can remember where I was going with this— is there's something in the Japanese psyche that positively revels in saying "don't," as opposed to, Oh I dunno, hanging your damn lamp a couple inches higher. Sorry, my bad. And there's apparently no end of the "don'ts." Don't get in the bathtub without showering first. Don't pour soy sauce on your rice. Don't assume that hot girl waiting for a bus wants to chat. So many small rules to be aware of. She was probably just having a bad day. Don't take it personally.

But with all the helpful advice Japanese people provide on a daily basis, somehow they neglected to mention the one thing you must never do in Japan: Don't leave a wet plastic bag of potatoes on your balcony for two weeks. Sure, maybe it'd be okay in winter, I don't know. I'm not a scientist. But in summer, I feel confident in saying that, whether you put on the balcony slippers or not, when you open that bag, it ain't gonna be good.

The fact is, I thought all those fruit flies were just from the plums. That would make sense, because I also had a bag of wet plums in the front hall. Not to mention the pumpkins, mushrooms, and zucchini. See, I got back from this Japanese farm a couple weeks ago, dripping with rain and struggling with my muddy boots, and I had craploads of crops. And not your neatly arranged farmer's market vegetables and fruits either. I'm talking a full crapload of produce. That's a lot. It's a technical term.

I'm not exactly crazy about working on the farm. But since I've got these Japanese friends who are farmers and they send me emails like, "Ken, when do you want to harvest with us?" there's not much I can do. I'm always like, How does "never" work for you? Farming involves two things I'm morally opposed to: mud, and hard work. It's common knowledge that civilization solved those problems back in the Dark Ages, over a hundred years ago. That's why we have the internet, so we don't have to use oxen and stuff. But since they're genuinely nice guys, I put on my boots and gloves and went to the farm again to plant some stuff and pick some other stuff. Who knows what it was, vegetable matter or something. And my buddies were invariably helpful, saying things like, "Don't hold the shovel like that, hold it like this," and "Don't get bit by snakes." Farming's great, let me tell you.

But the main problem with the farm, aside from horrible dirt and bugs, is all the crops I get. Farmer guys are always like, Want some onions? Great, here's a hundred. And I'm like, first of all, there's no way I can carry eighty pounds of onions home on the train, nor do I have the space to store them, and most of all I don't even cook because it's a pain in the ass. That's why I have a real job and I'm not a freaking farmer, to make money so I don't have to do stuff like that. But how you gonna say no? They're all like, but these are the delicious onions we all planted *together*. Here, take at least fifty. So I came home in the rain, on the train, with my onions and plums and all these other freaking crops, and got into my apartment and took off my muddy boots and put on my slippers and then took them off again when I reached the carpet and then started trying to stash all these wet bags of produce around my tiny apartment. I put a bunch out on the balcony, after carefully putting on a robe and changing into the balcony slippers, and a few dripping bags in the bathroom while wearing the appropriate bathroom slippers, before hopping into the tub after showing first.

Then over the next week I labored like Hercules cooking, freezing, and giving away crops to coworkers and random girls waiting for buses, until all I had left was a bag of plums. It took me till midnight, but I finally managed to submerge those fruity bastards in some white liquor to make Japanese plum wine, before collapsing onto my futon amidst a swarm of fruit flies. I took to blasting them with hair spray, which worked pretty well. My hair looked great too, although it sure did make the floor sticky. Well, there's some drawback to pretty much everything, I guess.

But they kept coming. They multiplied like, I dunno, some sort of winged insect. I was like, Where the hell are these coming from? They were everywhere, especially on the balcony. That's what eventually led me outside in my slippers and robe. And I have one piece of advice for anyone in Japan who discovers a wet bag of potatoes on his or her balcony: Don't look inside.

You know Pandora, like with the box and all? Yeah, well at least at the bottom she still had Hope. But when I opened my bag a hellish smell rushed out, and what I saw inside wasn't freaking that. It turns out you can produce something that looks and smells exactly like baby poo even without the actual baby. So full of mysteries, nature.

I threw off the robe and raced through my apartment still in the balcony slippers while grabbing every bottle of liquid available—Febreze, Listerine, soy sauce, plum wine, bleach— bleach, that's the ticket! I poured the contents of the bottle into the bag of potatoes. Of course, it should be immediately obvious to anyone that pouring bleach into a bag of rotting potatoes is a poor decision, but you know, hindsight and all. The smell got much, much worse, and the bag started oozing liquid something horrible. So I grabbed more bags. I put everything inside two other plastic bags. Then I double-bagged that. And still the smell continued. That's when I realized it wasn't trash day.

In Japan, you can't just throw out your trash whenever you want. There's a big sign in front of my apartment that says "Don't discard garbage on the wrong day." This essentially makes everybody's balcony into a personal trash collection facility. Like, it probably took my friend a month just to throw out her wine bottle and broken lamp. That's why I forgot about my potatoes, because they were buried under a bag of malt liquor cans on the balcony. See how complicated Japan is? It's not just me, I think.

So I decided to take my potatoes for a little walk. It may not be trash day in my neighborhood, but it's damn well trash day somewhere. But you know in Japan, you can't just go outside without looking good. Don't forget to shave. Don't wear a bathrobe. Don't stroll around with a sack that smells like baby shit. So many cultural mores. But there's also a Japanese solution for all that: the surgical mask. Got acne? No makeup? Socially inept because you grew up in this country? Yo, problem solved. I decided a beanie and some sunglasses might also be a nice touch, then set out amidst the salarymen in suits and women with small dogs with my terrible cargo. I am the veritable ambassador of good will.

I'm not going to tell you that I walked for two hours looking for a neighborhood in which it was trash day, sweating like a bonsai tree in a barbershop. I'm not going to say that I eventually tossed my stash into the garbage area of a large apartment complex two towns away and then set off running. Ken Seeroi in no way implicates himself in the dumping of toxic waste in Japan. Let's just say that the problem worked itself out, and the fruit flies have returned to normal levels.

Yeah, there's a lot of stuff you shouldn't do in Japan. I know because I've done most of it. But it's best not to dwell on the small things, because they just distract you from the big things you really shouldn't do anywhere. Like, well, farming. That's why God invented the restaurant. Which is where I went after another long shower and fresh application of hair spray, to my local *izakaya*. And looking at the menu, I briefly reviewed the list of what not to do: Don't pour soy sauce on the rice, don't start eating without saying *itadakimasu*, and sure as hell don't order the potato salad.

Japanese Fireworks, Better in Almost Every Way

Has it already been two weeks? Jeez, where does the time go? So yeah, a couple of weekends ago I went to a Japanese fireworks festival. Seems like only yesterday. At any rate, suffice to say watching fireworks in Japan is just like watching fireworks in the U.S., except better in every way. Well, except for one.

To start out with, you don't have to drive. You just put on your bathrobe, which is what Japanese folks call a *yukata*, but really it's a bathrobe, and your wooden sandals and get on the subway with about a million other people. Know how hard it is to walk down steps into the station wearing a bathrobe and flip-flops hewn from oak trees? Of course you don't, because you're not a grown man playing dress-up. You've gotta clutch the folds of your robe like a schoolgirl and try not to slip on the smooth granite. And who came up with making footwear out of wood anyway? Like, you never heard of Nike? Really need to work on that shoe technology, Japan.

As far as I can tell, the traditional thing to do when you arrive at a Japanese fireworks festival is to wander around in your bathrobe looking at your iPhone trying to locate your friends out of about two billion people. I was supposed to meet a young lady there. Actually, she's not that young, but hey, at least she's not a dude, so one out of two ain't bad. And while I was texting and trying not to trample someone else's picnic with my oaken clogs, I heard my favorite sound in the whole world, which is

"Want a beer?"

I like that so much. "Do I ever," I said instantly, and looked down to find a large blue plastic sheet full of guys and gals, all sitting silently. The thing about Japanese people is, frankly, they're pretty awkward in mixed company. They have the hardest time talking to each other, probably because they've never done it. Not real big on communication, the Japanese.

That's where I come in. Japanese people like to invite "foreigners" because, well, now there's something to talk about. Namely, my foreignness. It's like if we were a bunch of white folk all sitting around having a semi-un-fun picnic, and then suddenly a black guy came by. How entertaining would that be! To have a black guy join our picnic? It'd be awesome! Because, you know, he's black.

So I sat down and we all *kanpai*-ed, and they asked in stilted English where I was from and if I'd ever drunk Japanese sake and if I could use chopsticks until they figured out I actually lived in Japan and spoke Japanese, and it slowly became evident I wasn't some tourist to whom they could introduce the wonders of Japan, but rather just an ordinary dude from the next town over who was drinking all their booze. And then my lady friend found me and they were like Oh, you already have a Japanese friend, and then everyone seemed so disappointed and it became awkward again, so I figured maybe now was a good time to leave.

My lady friend and I set up our own plastic sheet next to a children's swing set under a tree. We had what in theater parlance would be termed a "semi-obstructed view," meaning that we could see the sky if we squinted hard and used our imaginations. There's a crazy amount of people at a fireworks festival, is what I'm trying to say. Then I asked her to wait for a minute and went off in search of deliciousness. I looked back and she was sitting contentedly on the sheet in her bathrobe, texting away. She looked pretty good, from that distance.

Food at a Japanese festival follows a theme. See if you can detect it. Rows of smokey booths offer up fried chicken, fried sausage, fried noodles, and stuff you never dreamed could be fried like, I dunno, cabbage and squid. Somehow that gets folded into savory pancakes, which are then fried, or the same pancakes with an egg on top, or the same pancakes wrapped around a hot dog and stuck on a stick. So much variety. Well, everything's good on a stick. That's one of the two truths of the universe.

The other being that everything tastes good fried. You gotta wonder what people did before, like back in the Pleistocene era.

"Hey, Grork, climb off that dinosaur and get over here."

"Yo Ken, what up?"

"Check out this new way of cooking lizard bone I just invented. I call it 'fried.'"

"Intriguing. Hmm. Light, yet crispy. Tastes like chicken. It'll go well with my new invention, beer. Let's have a festival."

"Great. If only there were some bright things we could shoot into the sky."

"How about just throwing a bunch of hot coals into the air with our hands?"

"Dude, genius. This'll be big someday."

Ah jeez, all the good stuff's already been invented. So I went back to my sheet by the swing set with a quiver of fried food and several cans of beer. That's another nice thing about Japan—you can drink outside like a normal adult and nobody's going to club you with a nightstick until you wake up behind bars. So that's advantage, Japan. Like when I lived in the U.S., it was easy to forget drinking outdoors violated some law the Pilgrims dreamed up, because it makes no sense. Tossing horseshoes while sipping a gin and tonic in the sunshine and fresh air, that's just healthy. Who doesn't like health?

Americans, apparently, which leads to some small, uh, misunderstandings, like ones where Ken Seeroi inconveniently winds up in jail. You mean we have to play horseshoes indoors? What am I, a lawyer—how am I supposed to remember so many rules? They say ignorance of the law is no defense. The hell—of course it is. That's like if you drink a beer on my balcony and I'm like, what the eff, dude, you can't drink out here. And you say, Sorry, nobody told me. Well, too bad, 'cause now we gotta lock you in the closet. Don't worry, I'll slide in baloney sandwiches and some grape drink at lunchtime.

But back to the festival, because about two beers later, the fireworks started. They were pretty identical to fireworks anywhere, with lots of loudness and bright lights and shapes of hearts, stars, and Hello Kitties. Only they just went on and on, for about an hour and a half. I was like, When's this shit over? After a couple minutes I'd pretty much gotten the concept. Good thing we had all that beer. Even still, I had to go back to the booths twice for more fried stuff on sticks. All that looking up sure makes a brother hungry.

And then it was over. One last ear-splitting ka-boom where they sent every flammable thing in their arsenal into the air at once and it was brighter than daylight and then suddenly the world fell strangely quiet. Then everybody jumped up in their bathrobes, tossed their beer cans and skewers into a tremendous trash pile and rushed for the subway. Which made me realize there's only one drawback to a Japanese fireworks festival—all those damned Japanese people. There sure are a lot of them. My lady friend and I crushed onto a subway car with about five hundred of our closest friends and I hung onto a strap and she hung onto me and we went to sleep standing up and dreaming we could breathe again. Next year, think I'll avoid the subway and try some place a little less crowded, like, I dunno, America. Man, that'd be sweet.

Is Japan Becoming a Muslim Nation?

Every spring, thousands of *sakura* trees bloom magnificently across Japan. And in synch, millions of Japanese folks don surgical masks, which they won't take off till winter, their allergies made exponentially worse by clouds of pollen blowing from the cherry blossoms and distant mountains of cypress.

"Years ago, we started chopping down the hardwood," Setsuko explained, "and replacing them with faster-growing conifers." That's my girlfriend with the runny nose. She knows a lot of stuff.

"Maybe you could not wear the mask while we're on dates?" I pleaded.

"But you hate my sniffling."

Point, Setsuko. "Well, how come nobody thought of that before all the chopping and planting?" I asked.

"Japan likes flowers and needs wood," she said, matter-of-factly.

"As do we all," I said. "In fact, I'm getting some now."

"Or maybe Japanese just aren't good at long-range planning."

"Looking at a map of Tokyo," I said, "you'd never guess."

Okay, tough segue, but here goes—See, for some reason, every time I check the news, there's another story about Muslims in Japan. Jeez, you search for something once, and Google News won't shut up about it.

These days, all over Japan, there are magazines for Muslim tourists, women in hijab strolling the streets of Okinawa, and halal food in Kyoto. It's like the opposite of Europe, where everyone's stressing over immigration. In Japan, people from Indonesia and the Middle East are actively recruited as workers and solicited by Japanese language schools. Hey, it's the new millennia. Being popular because you're white is so 1995.

So I was walking with my friend Baniti, who moved here from Egypt, and he asked, "Ken, are you still fasting?" And I was like Yeah, because I have no self-control. If I could stop at two beers and half a pizza, I wouldn't need to fast, but since dinners frequently consist of a six-pack, 2-for-1 Domino's, then running to the store for popcorn and malt liquor, I either have to avoid eating till noon or buy drawstring trousers.

"Great," he said, "Why don't you come by our house for Ramadan breakfast?"

"Wow, that'd be awesome." I said. "What time?"

"Four a.m."

"Scarily close to bedtime, but sure, I'm always up for something new. What's on the menu?" I'm thinking like breakfast burritos.

And Baniti's all, "Oh, you'll love it. We're having figs and milk."

"Figs and milk? My two favorite things," I lied. Looks like Ken's gonna need to rescue this breakfast. Wait till I introduce your family to thick & fluffy Eggo waffles.

Baniti's got two stunningly beautiful sons who go to Japanese school. And they're not the only kids in class with darker complexions. You don't need to be a prophet to figure that in a few years, Japan's gonna look a whole lot different than it does now. That'll probably be good.

See, this isn't about religion, but demographics. Let me impart three short stories about four friends: Stanley and his wife packed up and left Tokyo for Vietnam. "The food's spicier, the people nicer, and there are actually jobs with a future," he said. Robbie studied Japanese in college, spoke it fluently, and lasted three years in Yokohama. His final words were, "Enough with Japanese racism, I'm out." Bonnie moved back to San Francisco. "Dating in Japan sucks," she said. "My advice for women heading there would be, Buy a dildo." Ah, Americans. You have a solution for everything.

See, I told you they were short. But here are other stories. Like about the Afghani bartender at my corner izakaya, who's got two kids with a Japanese woman. And the students from Bangladesh on the train, all working like crazy to learn

Japanese and make a living here. And the Pakistani woman who attends my Thursday night Business English class. Throughout Japan, there are loads of Muslim people.

And nothing wrong with that, but it's a story that unfolds in numbers. Japan's population is taking a nose-dive. Counting on the Japanese to repopulate the nation? Tokyo'll be underwater before that happens. There's a steady influx of *gaijin* English teachers who show up believing that Japan's some mysterious Oriental land, then fly home two years later none the wiser. Meanwhile, masses of workers from India and the Philippines are migrating to a nation with better opportunities, and putting down roots.

So whither the future of Japan? More and more kids born with curly hair, is whither. If Japan makes it hard for Westerners to integrate (they just look so, you know, *different*), it seems to have less a problem with people from Muslim countries, who generally appear more Asian, provide great cheap labor and, uh, by the way, aren't leaving. Even now, the traditional "Japanese" appearance is shifting to include darker skin tones. Hey, I'm all for it so long as the number of delicious falafel restaurants continues to increase. Integration at last. I thought I was going to contribute to Japan's changing demographics, but watching the columns of workers from Nepal stream past on *mamachari* each morning, nah, I'm just a drop in the bucket. Good thing I like curry.

How to Talk to Gaijin: Advice for the People of Japan

Okay, here's what I've discovered does not work when meeting women. Gazing at them, silently but intently. Discussing their breasts. Touching them, pretty much anywhere. I know, you'd think these methods would be great, but somehow they aren't, which is weird. Let's not talk about how I know this.

So I was in a little Japanese bar the other day, just standing there having a glass of watery *shochu* and some chewy dried squid, when a short Japanese man positioned himself next to me. He just stood there, transfixed by my large white presence, and I wondered how long it'd take before he'd try out some English. I checked my watch.

To his credit, he had remarkable powers of concentration. Thirty seconds, a minute, minute ten, then finally, when he could contain himself no longer, out it came.

"Herroo!"

Japanese people are rather predictable in this respect.

I replied in Japanese, which is something of a self-protective reflex, like a *fugu* puffing up. "*Konnichiwa*," I said. Next, he'll ask where I'm from.

"Oh, your Japanese is so good," he said in Japanese. Whoops, forgot about that one.

"Want some squid?" I continued in Japanese, then took a big bite. "Izzz derishus."

"Where're you from?" he stammered. Okay, now I'm batting a thousand again. He started sweating profusely.

"Jus' down the street," I answered, chewing like mad. "Hawabout you?"

"No, no, what country? Where were you born?"

"Oh, uh, 'merica."

He grabbed my hand, started shaking it, and wouldn't let go. "I'm so glad to meet you," he said. "So glad."

"That's my squid-eating hand," I said.

207

I looked at him, then at my squid. Tears were welling in his eyes and he was shaking. I mean the Japanese guy. The squid was doing just fine, although granted, a bit dry. I wished I had some mayonnaise.

"Let's take a picture!" said the little man, and out came a phone.

"M'kay," I said, "jus' lemme finish chewing."

I must be in half the photo albums of Japan. I wonder if Japanese people ever get together and say, "Oh, that dude? Damn, I got a picture with him too!" Actually, I'm sure that happens.

I expect this is why women get breast reductions.

Now, to be honest, I might only be talking to you because I like how you look. That is, if you're a woman. It's like your personality can't even escape the gravity of your own hotness. Like you're an amazing goldfish saying all this brilliant stuff but trapped in a fishbowl and everyone's going, "Awww look, it's moving its little mouth, trying to say something." Yeah, sorry about that. Probably better if you're a guy, really, because then we can just talk about baseball or something. Actually, in that case, I can't notice how you look at all, because that's how people turn gay. So how 'bout them Dodgers?

What I've learned is you gotta be careful when conversing with women. Even if you're wearing a low-cut blouse, we have to talk about art or dogs or some nonsense. Your smoking-hot body isn't a good initial topic of conversation, unless maybe you've got implants, and then for some reason we can talk about them. But apparently women don't like random dudes blurting out how amazing they look any more than I do. It's all very confusing.

So to the nation of Japan, I've one simple request: Quit staring at my tits. And by "tits," I mean "whiteness," just to be clear. Sure, I do a lot of push-ups, but they're called "pecs," if you must know. And if I can't stare, then neither can you. So stop buying me drinks and gently touching my arm, cause y'all are creeping me out. At least pretend to like me as a person. You don't open a conversation with a visually-impaired person by remarking "Nice cane" or "You walk as well as a guy with eyes." So just do whatever you'd do if I looked "Japanese." Talk about sports or something. Okay, if you're a hot Japanese girl, maybe we can work something out. You tell me how well I use chopsticks and I'll laugh and pretend you're saying something intelligent while staring at your chest. See, now everybody's happy.

Mo' Money in Japan

Allow me to save you some reading time today, by giving you the conclusion up front. Because as any young lady who has visited my apartment can tell you, Ken Seeroi's all about time efficiency. Do the dishes? Wash clothes? Take a shower? Heh, that's just precious time better spent on more valuable things. Like, I dunno, enjoying champagne and fresh mango. Man, now that's a stellar combination. And chicks really dig it. But you gotta get them in season, that's the key. The mango, that is, not the women. Those are good year-round. But where were we? Oh right, money in Japan. Carry a freaking lot. Really, that's about it.

So I was in a Ginza Starbucks a few months ago, teaching an informal English lesson to a slightly overweight young student with long hair and a pretty smile. We were at a window seat, watching salarymen in suits rush by, when a girl passed in front of us carrying a plastic bag full of cash. Not like fifty dollars in nickels either; more like ten thousand dollars in yen. In a clear plastic bag. I'm guessing she was a store employee on her way to make a bank deposit, and her nonchalant attitude was pretty impressive, like, Ho hum, on my way to the bank with my huge bag of yen, oh there's a Starbucks, oh there's a fluffy dog, doot de doo...

I looked at my student. "Was that a bag full of yen?" I asked.

To which she replied, "You know, in Japanese, we say '*en*.'"

"Umm," I said, "let's not forget who's the English teacher here. It's pronounced 'yen,' with a 'Y.' And that was one huge pile of yen."

"*En*," she said.

Some people really need to learn how to let things go, jeez. Still, my point is: You won't be robbed in Japan.

Okay, maybe you will. Sure, anything's possible. Like you could walk under a ladder and a black cat'd fall on your head, but chances are, nobody's gonna jack you for your wallet or club you over the head with an iPad and steal your iPhone.

Don't be an idiot; but still, you're pretty safe.

Now let me say, when I lived in the U.S., the average amount of money I carried was about sixty cents. Because people in the U.S. have guns. So I debit-carded everything. Pack of gum? Here's a card. Six pack of beer, comb, Hershey's bar, and a copy of *Oui*? No, not that one, the Christmas edition. Put it on the card.

That doesn't fly here. Japan's a technologically-impaired nation twenty years late for the twenty-first century, where cash is still king. Sure, if you stay at the Hyatt Regency and eat every meal at Denny's, you can use plastic, but for most stuff on a daily basis, you need that paper, and plenty of it. Which means: Japan's the greatest country ever for robbers.

Japanese people carry a ton of cash, seriously. Most folks have over $200 in their wallets at any given time. In yen, that is. I'll just use "dollars" from now on so you don't have to bust out a calculator for the exchange rate, but really, we're talking yen. Either way, if ever there was a country where a petty thief could make a great living, it'd be Japan. Not that I'd recommend it. After all, you'd do better teaching English to plump girls in Ginza Starbucks while tempting them to visit your apartment stocked full of cheap champagne and seasonal mangos.

There are times I look in my wallet and think, Wow, I'm carrying like six hundred bucks. That's a little dangerous, since I'm going out tonight. Better get a couple hundred more. So my advice to anyone visiting or living in Japan, but especially visiting, is: Carry a shit-ton of Japanese folding money.

Practically, that's at least two hundred bucks. I mean, in yen. Or *en*. Or whatever, because you can't spend dollars. Why carry so much? Let me give you a few scenarios drawn from the experiences of a close friend of mine, also coincidentally named Ken.

1. Ken, newly arrived in Japan, goes out to eat, but doesn't completely understand what he sees on the menu. He orders

a beer that's three feet tall, a salad made from an entire raw onion, and a selection of tempura suitable for a family of six. Then when the bill comes, he's drunk as hell, has horrible breath, and is approaching heart failure from the buildup of saturated arterial fat. About that time, he realizes he doesn't have enough money to cover the bill. This is not well received by the restaurant staff.

2. Ken goes to a bar. This time he has enough money. Then at the bar, he makes a bunch of new friends, which is great, since Ken likes friends. And they want to hang out with him, because he's such a cool guy. Or because he's white. So they take him to a karaoke bar, which is also great, since Ken believes himself to be a most excellent singer when drunk. Then after three hours of drinking beer, eating snacks which appear free, and singing Japanese folk songs, his new friends decide it's time to settle the bill and sprint for the last train. And about this time Ken realizes that while he had enough money at the beginning of the night, somehow it's all mysteriously disappeared. This is not well-received by Ken's former new friends.

3. Ken, now carrying a massive extra cushion of cash, goes out to a different bar where people don't yet hate him. He enjoys a pleasant evening of modest drinking, restrained karaoke, and makes it to the station with plenty of yen left and time to spare before the last train. Okay, maybe he stops to get one last tallboy of malt liquor at the convenience store before heading to the station, but either way, he's still got more than enough money to get home. So he boards the train, and just as the doors close, he realizes, Shit, wrong train. And that train turns out to be an express straight to Saitama and it's the last train and now it's 1:30 a.m. and Ken's in dark and scary Saitama and there's no way back home except for a fifty dollar taxi ride, which exceeds the amount of money in Ken's wallet by about forty-nine. Ken is perplexed by this situation, but drinks the malt liquor, since maybe that'll make things clearer, and anyway it looks like it's going to be a long night.

4. Ken, pockets now bursting with yen, is stumbling home late one evening through the red-light district, by accident, of course. Then, walking past a club, a doorman asks if he'd like to have a beer and talk to some pretty girls. Ken says no, because he's not that kind of guy. He's a serious and upright individual, with principles. Thirty seconds later, Ken's on a velvet couch, glass in hand, surrounded by a crush of pretty women. Good times! He sings a bunch of karaoke and everyone tells him what an excellent singer he is. But Ken's no idiot, so he only has two beers. Well, maybe three, and buys one or two for the girls, but still. Finally, he gets up to leave and is presented with the bill, which is more than his monthly rent. Suddenly, the doorman who was so nice has been replaced by a totally scary yakuza thug. Again, Ken's situation is less than well-received.

Look, I live this stuff so you don't have to, so just carry way more cash than you think you need. Also know that Japanese ATMs have the bizarre tendency to be closed when you most need them, like late at night when accompanied by the yakuza. You're all like, how could an automated machine be closed? But the yakuza don't want to hear that. Pointing out what a stupid country Japan is will not improve the situation.

Now, I don't want to give the impression Japan's expensive. It can be much cheaper than the U.S., if you understand the system. A beer can cost you ten dollars, or two dollars, depending on the choices you make. So until you can speak, and especially read, Japanese with a fair degree of competence, the chances of screwing up and having to fork out extra bucks is pretty high. And since you can't always fall back on credit cards, problems are likely to arise, to put it mildly.

Finally, know there's no shortage of crime in Japan. Two of my students had their purses snatched while walking at night, and another friend had her wallet stolen. Home break-ins are also pretty popular. This nation's not immune to petty larceny, although probably less than most places. Except Switzerland, but all they eat is cheese with holes, so don't go there. Regardless, you're more likely to run into problems not carrying enough cash rather than too much. Just don't go strolling at night with a clear bag full of the stuff. Wait till daytime. Mo' money, no problems. That's how we roll in Japan.

Japan's Renegade Turtles

So I'm heading to work early one morning when I happen to glance down and see this little Japanese turtle right in the middle of the road, totally random. Sure, okay, I couldn't really tell if he was a Japanese turtle or a *gaijin* turtle, but he had the shell and the stubby reptile legs and all, so I felt pretty good about the turtle part. And he was escaping from this neighborhood reservoir, full of green water and surrounded by tall chain link fence. How a turtle got over a seven foot-high fence, I'll never know, but it seems he was one of those super ninja turtles. You never can tell in this country.

So here I am half-running in my suit, trying to get to the station because I'm late as usual, without breaking too much of a sweat, and suddenly there's this little guy struggling to get across the road. Why, I have no idea. I guess to get to the other side, like a reaaally slow chicken. But I kept going, because I had a train to catch, and there were about a million other people in suits rushing by who could deal with the situation.

And then it occurred to me. Japanese turtle or not, nobody's going to help. Like, the entire nation's going to pass by, look at him, and not do a damn thing. And then he'll be crushed by a car or that truck that drives around picking up discarded TVs and bicycles. I mean, it's a busy road. Jeez, why does it always fall on the white guy to do everything? But okay, yeah, it does, so I went back.

Have you ever seen a Japanese superhero? No, right? Unless you're really into anime or something, but otherwise the answer's likely No. The whole world knows Superman, but who's Japan got? Godzilla? He's just a big, walking crocodile. And his pal Gamera, who's basically a giant turtle. Which is my point exactly—what kind of place has a turtle and crocodile for national symbols? Japan's so orderly that the demand for superheroes is really low. So if Superman ever did visit Japan, he'd just be stuck doing all this boring, petty stuff like saying, Don't throw your cigarette butts down the drain! or separating the recycling into glass, cans, and plastic, only really fast. He'd probably be Super-annoyed man, actually. Not that I'm trying to say I'm like Superman or anything. I'm just some dude hustling to work so I can get the whole teaching English thing out of the way in order to come back home and drink a proper beer. That's it. On the other hand, I guess from the turtle's perspective, well okay, maybe I am. Not that I'm boasting, but I'm a lot taller than he is, for starters. By night, an English teacher, and by day, turtle Superman. That's gotta look good on a resume. Oh, life's turning out just dandy.

So I picked him up. You know how some people collect snakes or have an ant farm or like to hug sheep? Yeah well, that ain't Ken Seeroi. I was like, Eeeew, how do I hold this gross thing? He was all moving and alive and stuff, but thankfully he pulled his scary little legs and head back into his shell, so that helped. I could kind of imagine he was just like a hubcap or something. But then he started peeing. So now a million Japanese people are rushing by and here's this white guy in a suit standing in the middle of the road holding a whizzing turtle and pretending he's a hubcap. It's a good thing I wore blue, and not my grey pinstripe. Hides the turtle pee much better.

Then Mr. Turtle got the ride of his life. I carried him back to the reservoir and chucked him over. I was like, Be free, little turtle, fly! Only I kind of threw him too far, and for a moment I was afraid he'd sail entirely over the reservoir and splat onto the road on the other side, which would be pretty ironic. I've really got a hell of an arm, I must say. But eventually he came back down and hit the water in a massive belly flop. There was a great splash, and slowly he disappeared below the surface. Back to his watery home. I don't care if you've got a shell or not though, that's gotta sting. Afterwards, I started worrying that maybe he'd been a tortoise, and I'd just drowned him, which'd be even more ironic. But hey, you can't account for every contingency.

Then I slotted back into the line of people rushing to the

station, and washed my hands of the whole matter. Meaning that I stopped at the restroom and rinsed off the turtle slime, then got onto the train and pulled out my smartphone like everybody else. Faceless and anonymous Clark Kent blending in with the masses, texting his boss that he's late, pants already drying nicely, patiently waiting for the next time he's gonna save the world.

Homeless in Japan Not Big Fans of America

Last Friday, I decided to celebrate the lovely fall weather by drinking a refreshing beer in my neighborhood park and working on my tan. I've discovered this really beats the hell out of sitting in a smoky *izakaya* wishing the proprietor'd had the foresight to provide some outdoor seating or at least install a teeny tiny window. Why the Japanese have such an aversion to open-air dining, I've never understood. So full of mysteries, the Far East.

Then just as I was dreaming of how good I was gonna look with my new golden skin color, I noticed a homeless guy sitting across from me, on a piece of cardboard, on the ground. He was drinking one of those cheap 100-yen cups of rot-gut *shochu*, and looked in desperate need of a bath. Well that's cool, I figured, public park. Plus I hadn't exactly showered this morning either. Hey, I was busy. So I figured there was no reason we couldn't both enjoy a pleasant cocktail after a hard day of teaching English or rummaging through garbage for aluminum cans. I'm generous with my park like that.

He looked over at me. I nodded and raised my beer. To which he replied in loud English, "America fuck you!"

That rather caught me off guard. My first thought was, Whoa, where's this coming from? Like I get some minor racism in Japan on a daily basis, but it's usually subtle. Like maybe somebody hands me a fork instead of chopsticks, that kind of thing. This lacked such nuance, and my second thought was, "Shouldn't there be punctuation somewhere in that sentence?" But before I could point that out, he launched into a stream of English invectives, basically every swear word you've ever heard, and concluded with:

"Go back U.S.A.! Here's Japan! We hate you!"

Then he spit in my direction.

Well, that did it. You know, Ken Seeroi's a basically pretty mellow dude. After all, avoiding stress is how I maintain my youthful and radiant skin tone. And you thought it was just a daily regimen of Oil of Olay. But hey, even I've got my limits. Cuss me out? What, are you trying to ruin my complexion? But okay, I can deal with that. Spit at me? Eh, all right, since you're twenty feet away, that doesn't really phase me. But insult America? Okay now you've...well, mmm, all right, you've got a point. I did move to Japan, after all, so I can't really talk. But speak English just because I'm white? Oh, now you've done gone too far. There's only so much a brother can reasonably tolerate.

So I said back at him in Japanese, "We need to work on your grammar." But I said it without using the polite verb ending, just to let him know how I really felt. Take that, you.

This in turn set him off, and he resumed his string of English cuss words, interspersed with references to World War Two, the U.S. Army, Hiroshima, and, for some reason, the iPhone.

"Made in China, my friend," I replied in Japanese.

Despite his grammar, I had to admit he had an impressive vocabulary of inventively vulgar language. He swore like a sailor. Although, granted, I've never actually spoken to a sailor. What about the sea makes them so angry? Remind me to re-read Moby Dick.

And so we continued in this vein for some time, enjoying the fall weather, taking our respective sips of beer and *shochu*, and ranting incomprehensibly. Jeez, if there's one thing I can't stand when I go for a drink in the park, it's some drunk wrecking the place. I mean other than me, of course.

But the whole time, he wouldn't stop yelling at me in English, which seemed a bit culturally insensitive. We're in Japan, for eff's sakes—couldn't you at least insult me in Japanese? That's only polite. Then to make matters worse, I eventually ran out of equivalent Japanese insults, which left me at a disadvantage. Is it my fault English is such a rich language for swearing? I blame the French. So I figured it was time to Phone a Friend, and I knew just who to call.

Makiko's easily the meanest Japanese girl I know, and given the women of this nation, that's saying something. Just three semi-unrelated facts to help paint the picture: Makiko's brother's a Yakuza, she previously worked in the "adult entertainment" industry, and in high school she used to sell her used panties for cash. All of which makes her awesome on so many levels. Hey, if you want my unwashed boxers, they're yours for a twenty. Just give 'em back clean and folded. On the flip side, she once got so mad she yanked open my apartment window and hurled my Starbucks tumbler onto the pavement, shattering it. To be fair, those do break really easily. Guess I shouldn't have told her about that episode with her roommate. Still, it cost me like ten bucks to replace. I called her on my iPhone.

"I've got, um, like a situation," I said to her in Japanese.

"What's wrong?" she said immediately. "Where are you? I'll be right there." And the way she said it, it sounded more like, "Whose ass do I need to kick?" God, she's mean. I love that about her, sometimes.

"There's this homeless guy in the park and he's yelling at me," I said, and suddenly I felt like I was five years old.

"Why don't you just leave?" she asked, which was a strangely reasonable suggestion. Did not anticipate that.

"Leave?" I said, "I can't do that. That would make too much sense. Then he'd win."

"I see," she said. "Well, why don't you swear back in English? That'd shut him up."

"English?" I said, "Ah shit, that's no good. I need like the worst Japanese insult you've got."

"Well, why don't you tell him: 'Die!'"

"Die?" I said. "That's the worst you've got?"

"That's what I'd say."

"I was really looking for something, y'know, a bit more gangster."

"Okay," she said, "then how about, 'Die, octopus!'"

"Die, octopus? I'm being cussed a new asshole by a guy who sleeps in a cardboard box and that's what you recommend I tell him?"

"That's a good one," she said. "I use it all the time."

"True," I acknowledged. I've heard it plenty.

Then I hung up and the homeless guy and I went back to drinking and glaring and occasionally yelling about the atomic bomb and the presence of U.S. troops in Okinawa in loud voices. But after a while I realized the sun was going down and the prime tanning hours were over, so I got up to leave.

"Enjoy your box," I said in Japanese.

"Go home, *gaijin*," he replied in English, and spit in my direction again.

"This is my home," I answered in Japanese, and started walking away. After all, who argues with a homeless guy in the park? Well, apparently I do, but still, better to take the high road, right? Right. Or at least the road straight to the convenience store. Because I was out of beer, so I figured I'd head in for a freshie. He was still yelling as I left, so just for good measure, I turned around and shouted back in Japanese, "Oh yeah? Well, die, octopus!" You know that's gotta sting. Then I went across the street to 7-Eleven, and when I came out it was dusk and I couldn't see across the park anymore. The moon was out, almost full, and I remembered what a lovely season fall is in Japan. But some days here, jeez. I just thank Japanese God this one was a Friday.

The Truth About Sex in Japan

Ah, sex in Japan, always a hot topic in online forums. If you're a man and you post, "I'm having lots of sex in Japan!" then someone will surely reply, "The women you're seeing are all hoes."

Or if you're a woman and post the same thing, then it's, "You yourself are a ho." That's what's known as a double standard. Is it just me who thinks the rise of the internet correlates directly with the decline of civilization? Eh, probably.

On the other hand, if you're a guy and post, "Japan sucks and I'm not having any sex," then someone will say," You're such a loser, since there are so many hoes." Or, if you're a woman: "You're still a ho."

Well, you can't argue with logic.

This rather banal discussion recently took a turn for the interesting, however, after the Japan Family Planning Association reported that 45% of young Japanese women, and over 25% of men, "were not interested in or despised sexual contact." *The Guardian* followed this with a piece entitled "Why have young people in Japan stopped having sex?"

So why have they?

After living here for a few years, this actually makes sense. Okay, I'm not like a sociologist or anything. I'm just some dude in Japan who tries to find a clean pair of socks so he can put one on and run to the station to cram onto the train with ten thousand of the unhappiest Japanese people you've ever seen. I don't pretend to have discovered the Unified Field Theory of Japanese sexuality, but I'll give you four factors I think are contributing.

Thing One: Work

People in Japan, and Tokyo in particular, work a ridiculous amount, in a way that's hard to comprehend if you live in, say, sunny California. Take a former student of mine, Nagisa, who had a job as a programmer. She worked—wrap your head around this—twenty hours a day.

"Every day at 4 a.m.," she said, "they'd turn off the lights and we'd sleep at our desks for four hours."

"Did you have locker rooms?" I asked. "What about clothes?"

"I just wore the same clothes, but on Sunday I'd go home for half a day, to shower. The men only went home once a month."

"That must have smelled pretty nice. How long'd you do that for?"

"Five years and three months," she said.

Okay, so maybe that's an extreme example. A more typical case is probably my former student Masahiro, who's an executive at a famous beverage manufacturer. He works from 9 a.m. until to midnight, six days a week, with a 15-minute lunch break at his desk. He has Sunday off, which is when he studies English.

"I have it easy," he said, "since I work at an international company. Japanese places are a lot worse."

"Do you ever see your wife?" I asked.

"I see her on Sunday," he said.

"But Sunday's when you come here to study English," I noted.

"Ah, good point," he said.

For most people, it comes down to two choices: work like mad as a single person and have a tiny apartment full of dirty clothes and half-eaten Cup Ramen containers, or get married. That way, the man goes off to work, and when he comes home after midnight, his dinner is sitting on the table covered in Saran Wrap, and there's hot water in the tub. His wife and daughter are already asleep. Shopping, ironing, cleaning, paying the bills, everything's taken care of for him. All he has to do is bring home a paycheck. The woman gets to do all the fun, fulfilling things like taking care of baby, grocery shopping, cleaning, and cooking meals. Sometimes I'll ask my adult students how often they see their spouses, or ask the kids when they see their fathers. The answer's roughly on par with how often I've seen a lunar eclipse. Although if you spend a lot of evenings drinking in the park, you'd be surprised at all the weird stuff in the sky, so maybe not as infrequent as you think.

The young Japanese people of today grew up watching their parents live that life, and it's understandable if they're not thrilled about it. Marriage isn't a great choice; it's just the second-worst option. For a man, it means he's working to pay for his wife. For a woman, it means a life of indentured servitude. A lot of people have decided to "just say no."

Thing Two: Prostitution

This may be challenging to reconcile if you don't live in Japan, but being in a relationship and having sex have precious little to do with one another. For a Japanese male, it's possible to get sex almost anywhere, at any time, for little more than the price of a decent lunch. Anyone who's been in Japan even a short while has seen the rows of shops offering all the usual services. (As an aside, I'll add that "foreigners" are generally barred from entry. You can be that unwashed dude who lives under a bridge and rides a bicycle with garbage bags full of tin cans hanging off the back, but as long as you appear "Japanese," you're a welcome customer. But Japanese racism's a whole other subject.)

Now, I'm in no way saying that the majority of men and women participate in this, but, well okay, a lot do. The fact the institution exists at all changes the social dynamic. Every Japanese person innately recognizes that:

If you're a man with just a little bit of money, you can have sex with as many attractive women as you want.

and

If you're an attractive woman, well...Look, I teach English for a living. Every week, people pay me to sit in Starbucks and simply talk with them. Afterwards, I go to a bar, and every week, sure as hell, someone will approach me and say, "Wow, let's speak English together!" Now, I may even want to, but really, who gives away what they can sell? It's my job, not my hobby.

So prostitution has turned sex in Japan into a commodity. It's something available for purchase, like movie tickets or a haircut or a bag of carrots. Sex isn't an expression of love between two people; it's something bought or sold when necessary.

Now, I don't actually know how many men and women frequent these places, or the number employed there. But from the billboards advertising busty women and pretty boys lit above neon alleys packed with customers every night, it sure seems a freaking lot. And because prostitution is so commonplace, it changes the way people view relationships. As in, I once dated a girl who told me, "You know, a lot of men would pay good money to be dating a woman like me." And I was like, Bitch, you're getting free English lessons. That's a thirty-dollar value.

Thing Three: Japanese Social Relations

Recently, a friend of mine got married to a man through an arranged marriage. She used to get drunk and make out with me whenever my girlfriend ran to the bathroom. She was great like that, actually.

"Do you love him?" I asked.

"He does train maintenance," she said. "That's a stable job."

"I'm pretty sure you just answered a different question," I said.

"Well, I will eventually," she replied.

I'll try to put this in the best light possible, but Japanese social relations are...um, well, they're *terrible*. Okay, that didn't come out so well. Abysmal? No, that's worse. Well, I'll come up with a more nuanced word and edit it in later.

The society functions with robot-like efficiency because your boss tells you what do—or your parents, or your teacher—and you do it. There's a hierarchy. If you're the cook in a ramen shop, you don't say, "Hey boss, how about if, instead of two slices of pork on the noodles, we tried *three*?" Are you insane? That's not how things work. The fact is, you don't challenge what you're told, you don't offer up original ideas, and you don't initiate conversations with strangers. Which presents a *koan*-like riddle: If you don't talk to people you don't know, how do you get to know anyone?

I've lived in my current apartment building for, let's see, about a year and a half now. Man, time flies. And in that time the number of neighbors I've met is...zero. I actually rode the elevator down with a guy yesterday. He was about my age and was tying his tie while I was still fumbling into my shoes. Okay, so here's a quiz for you, to see how well you understand Japanese culture:

I figured I'd break the ice with a non-threatening situational observation, so I said in Japanese:

"Yeah, another busy morning, huh?"

To which he replied (choose one):

a. "Mmm, sure is."

b. "Oh jeez, I can't believe my alarm didn't go off."

c. "Do you know how to tie a double Windsor?"

d. "Holy crap, a white guy in my building!"

If you chose e. "Absolutely freaking nothing," then congratulations, you're halfway to a Bachelor's in East Asian Studies. The reality is people don't have a lot of contact with each other. For Japanese folks, it's insanely difficult to establish friendships and connections. That's why so many Host and Hostess Bars exist, so you can at least pay someone to talk to you.

Japanese people excel at social interactions when there are clearly defined roles: Boss and Worker, Clerk and Customer, Drunk salaryman and *gaijin*. There are obvious rules and precedents for those situations. But for two Japanese people to strike up a conversation in line at the grocery store? Well, it's hypothetically possible, I suppose, like Dark Matter or something.

Thing Four: Japan's Sexy, Sexy Atmosphere

People are massively impacted by their environment and the people around them. That's the Ken Seeroi Theory of

Human Behavior. Wikipedia it. That means if everyone else is having an awesome, sexy time, you're more likely to as well. Which is why New Year's Eve exists. When it's a sunny day, everybody's happy, and when it rains, everybody's glum. Life's funny like that.

So I was talking this over with my colleague Fujimoto-sensei last week, and he said,

"Ah, Ken, you should have seen it in the 90's. Japan was different then. Everybody was making money, people were positive, it was more fun."

To which I replied, "Uh, it's '*Seeroi*-sensei,' remember? But yeah, I've heard that from a lot of people."

"Sorry, Ken-*sensei*," he said. Then, "You know I used to have a wife and a girlfriend in those days."

"And now all you have is a wife?" I asked.

"Yeah," he sighed. "I think we're in a recession."

So after work, I went to my usual *shokudo*, which is basically like a cheap restaurant. It's dingy and run-down, but the food's solid. I think of it like an extra living room, which helps since my apartment's so darn small. The place was packed with about thirty guys and gals in dark suits all sitting alone in silence, eating and reading manga or staring at their smartphones with glazed eyes. I stayed for about an hour and a half, ate some grilled mackerel and rice and miso soup, drank an Asahi beer, and watched TV. Their grilled fish is really good, I must say. The only person I talked with was the waitress, which is pretty typical. She's about sixty and doesn't say stupid things like, "Wow, you can use chopsticks," so I like her. Then I walked the concrete corridor alone to the station and joined the herd on the platform, silently waiting in line for the train.

When it came, it was packed as always, so we put on our faces of resignation and forced ourselves on since we had to, then rode without a word. When I got to my neighborhood it was dark, which was fine since there's really not much to see anyway, nothing like a river or a tree or anything. Well, there

227

is a little brown canal nearby, so I guess that's something. I stepped around some puddles on the asphalt as I walked past the same gray public housing I do every day, and thought, there must be a thousand units, and someone living in each one. Why is it I never see anyone on a balcony or in a window? And suddenly that seemed kind of strange, but then the feeling passed.

Eventually I got to my own dark building and rode the elevator up. Did I simply come to Japan too late? Like by twenty or thirty years? Then I opened the door and found my apartment just as I left it, full of dirty laundry and half-eaten Cup Ramen containers. Nah, Japan's still wonderful, I thought as I took a can of malt liquor from the fridge and sat on the floor. I just need a Japanese wife–that's the ticket. That, and a chair. Yeah, someone to clean this place up, cook me some hot meals, and love, eventually.

The 9 Best Things About Japan

Also known as, "Why on Earth am I Still Here?"

Well, the bad news is, I shattered a wine glass all over my new carpet last night. The good news is, hey, I got a new carpet. See, there's a bright side to everything.

So today I woke up with the window wide open and this terrifying headache and did a quick systems check. Do I have on underwear? Apparently so. Are they my own? Hmm, pink and satiny, yep, those'd be mine. Is anyone beside me? Perhaps she left to buy a vacuum cleaner. Do I have many small pieces of glass embedded in my feet? Sure feels like it. Oh God, why am I still in Japan? Then I looked at the clock and Whoa, no time for that—McDonald's breakfast service ends in nine minutes! I still can't figure out why it's physically impossible to drop a frozen hash brown into boiling oil after 10:30 a.m., but obviously it is. Ah, science, always so many new horizons to explore.

Well, there's nothing like an Egg McMuffin to clear your head, that's what I always say. All that cholesterol does wonders for the old cranial arteries. So while I was hunched over my molded yellow table trying to decide if I was having a stroke, hangover, or both, I briefly drifted into this flashback of coming to Japan for the first time, in which I played the part of Dorothy landing in Oz—everything was weird and funny and there were all these midget people running around. I had a band of friends with no brains or hearts, none of us could read or say anything that made sense, and everything we did was wrong. All that was missing was the mangy little dog, although there were plenty of stray cats. My first week, I went jogging and couldn't find my hotel again. I got on an elevator and a guy in a suit spontaneously hugged me. People helped me dress myself, showed me how to eat, and taught me how to use the toilet. It was awesome.

Nothing stays new forever though. Eventually the Yellow Brick Road ended and I could order my own soggy eggplant in restaurants. Then I stopped getting on the train going the opposite direction. At some point I figured out how to change the channel on the TV and quit talking to people with my hands in my pockets. Men stopped hugging me. I do kind of miss that.

But although Japan has become familiar, there's still a lot I don't know. Now, I'm sure you're saying, What, Ken Seeroi not know something? And yes, I too find it difficult to believe, but there you have it. For example, I still don't know the name of the street I live on after a year and a half. I'm starting to suspect it doesn't actually have a name. Though if it does, you can bet it's not gonna be Maple Avenue or something. More like 紅葉通り—See, impossible. Not my fault.

So that's part of what keeps me here—the remaining Mysteries of the Orient. Like, say, my washing machine. I'll be damned if I'm going to leave Japan before I figure out when to add the fabric softener. But that's just me. I like soft clothes. At the same time, the U.S. seems increasingly bizarre. What kind of a country has no public transportation? And don't say, "Uh, the bus?" because I rode one of those once and it just drove in circles around town. And where else in the world is it legal to carry a gun, but you get arrested for walking down the street with a beer? Why is there no permit allowing me to strap a spare Asahi to my ankle? I promise I won't use it unless provoked.

Which is to say that if I now see the downsides to Japan— the concrete poured over the hillsides, the power lines crisscrossing every picture of a temple I try to take, the waitresses who ask if I can eat sashimi because I'm, you know, white—I also know no place is perfect. Well okay, maybe Finland. But then you'd have to cross-country ski everywhere and wear like a reindeer suit, so that's out. Gotta draw the line somewhere. Although I could seriously rock some deer horns. But really, all countries, and all things, have good and bad, and I accept that. Donuts are delicious but fattening. Old men are wise but have hairy backs. Girls with big boobs have big butts.

That's just how God made the universe. Hey, first try so, well, A for effort.

Then there are the practical considerations. Leaving Japan isn't that easy. Probably should've thought about that before moving here, but eh, I'm not real big on planning. I enjoy surprises. So now—surprise—I've got a crapload of stuff: a comfy couch, rice cooker, and a miniature motorcycle. Not to mention an apartment, job, new carpet that glitters like glass, and more girlfriends than I can shake a stick at. Trust me, I've tried. Remarkably unflappable, Japanese women. On top of that, I hate cleaning and packing because they resemble work which I'm allergic to, so that alone is enough to keep me from moving forever. Then I'd have to buy a plane ticket for about a thousand bucks I don't have and when I got the States I'd have to live under a bridge until Walmart hired me because I've now got a giant Japan-sized hole on my resume. So it's not easy to just pack up and move, is what I'm saying.

And if I did move back to America, I doubt I'd ever visit Japan again. Why would I, really? Pay tons of money for a plane ticket, hotel rooms, train passes, food—all for like two weeks? Hell, I'm already here; why not just stay a couple weeks longer?

I'd almost certainly not live here again. It took a lot of time, cash, and effort to get set up in this crazy country. I can't really see dismantling all that—quitting my job, giving away my microwave with all the buttons I still don't understand, saying tearful goodbyes to everyone—and then coming back a year later, like Just kidding! Now can I please have my tiny apartment back?

Then there's the language. I don't like to say that I wasted fifteen years of my life studying Japanese. Instead, I prefer *invested* fifteen years of my life, because it sounds much better. Phraseology is everything. The truth is learning Japanese has been ridiculously time-consuming, moderately interesting, and even marginally useful. And now that I've gotten to the point where I can finally use the telephone without paralyzing fear, it seems a shame to scrap the whole project. If I'd learned Spanish, I could travel to a dozen countries with it. Or French, at least I could go to Quebec. But Japanese? It's basically here or nothing, and why keep working on the language after giving up on the country? Well, at least I can now order sushi like a boss anywhere on earth, so that's something. You should hear me pronounce "*edamame*." Like angels singing.

After you've been here for about a year, maybe two, well, things change. Japan stops being a foreign country and just becomes, what? home? It's not like you're living in a hotel forever, even if the room's the same size. The tourist attractions that were so fascinating at first become an everyday background, until you find yourself walking through Kyoto with a friend and you're like,

"Whoa, look at that!"

"Yeah sure, a ten-thousand-year-old temple encrusted with pure gold. Been there, so what?"

"No, fool, behind it—a Kentucky Fried Chicken!"

"Daaamn. They have a new seasonal menu! Let's go take photos with Colonel *ojisan*."

So that Japanesey stuff—all the geisha, karate, robots, maid café bullshit—it's not real life in Japan to me anymore, just some bizarre thing I read about on the internet. Like no way I'm taking a picture of a sumo wrestler; I'm more interested in bumping him out of the way so I can get a seat on the train. Hit low and catch them off balance, is my advice. Still, there are a few things I love about Japan, and that I'd really miss if I left.

The 9 Best Things About Japan

1. The food's amazing. You can get sushi at any 7-Eleven that puts to shame a fifty-dollar dinner in the U.S. None of that California roll and week-old fish people rave about in the States. Then there's the restaurant I stop at after work, where everyone says "Welcome home, Seeroi-san." Well, they don't actually verbalize it, but I know that's how they feel. It's like

my house, if my mom had been both Japanese and hated vacuuming. So it's a little shabby. But I can get a full, home-cooked meal for around six bucks. That's everything—food, drinks, tax, and no tip. Probably helps if you like Japanese home-cooking though. You're gonna have a hard time locating your beloved meatloaf, spinach dip, and green bean casserole.

2. Okay, just the entire dining experience. Like, ever have a waitress come to your table just as you shovel in a mouth-load of food and ask, "So, how's everything, hon?" Not in Japan you didn't. Here if you need something, you call for it, and if you don't, they leave you the hell alone as God intended. And when you do ask for, say, a beer—Boom, it just comes. Like in ten seconds. Why the same exact request takes ten minutes in the U.S., I've never been able to fathom.

3. Japan's cheap. You can live in a clean, safe apartment in a reasonable neighborhood of Tokyo for 800 bucks a month. Or cut that in half if you live in a smaller city. I'm trying to imagine the rat-filled hellhole I'd rent in like Chicago or Seattle for $400 a month, and it's pretty terrifying. Of course, if you want to live in a big place it's gonna cost you more. So just live in a small place, is what I figure. That's just less I have to clean. I mean, hypothetically, should I ever decide to.

4. The trains. You don't need a car. So I was talking to an American friend of mine about this and he said, "No, I like driving." Now, I feel that. I like the *idea* of whipping through the ocean spray as my tires grip the surface of a winding Pacific highway—that sounds great, but it's a car commercial. The reality is I'm sitting in traffic for hours plotting to murder the person who cut me off while badly needing to pee. So that's a lot less great. Then there's the hundreds of thousands of dollars that buying, maintaining, and insuring cars costs throughout one's lifetime. Money which could be spent on something more useful, like beer, which you can then drink plenty of and safely pass out on the train ride home. That's known as symbiosis.

5. National health insurance. Even when I took a few months

off from work (okay, maybe like a year), it only cost twenty bucks a month and I could still go to the doctor. Sure, maybe with Obamacare I could go to a public health center in the U.S., if death or prison were my other options. Actually, I'd choose prison because it's less scary. Like I was in this clinic in San Francisco and everyone was crowded into one giant waiting room for hours. Somebody big on planning had thoughtfully equipped the place with exactly nine chairs for a hundred people, and so finally, when this enormous fat lady left her seat and walked out of the room, I sat down. Then she came back and screamed "That's my seat!" I jumped up and started for the emergency exit. Jeez fatty, have your plastic chair already.

6. So I guess I'd have to add that Japanese folks aren't obnoxious. They generally dress like adults (even the kids), have fewer tattoos than a carny Ferris wheel operator, and don't reek of cologne. They even have a reputation for being polite (basically a massive PR campaign enlisting every Japanese person to remind you, "We're polite, you know"), although I wouldn't go that far. They have plenty of ways of being rude, but at least they do it freaking quietly. Even the minor put-downs seem almost innocent just because they're delivered so delicately. "Oh, you can eat rice crackers and drink green tea—*sugoi*!" Really, that impresses you? Just wait till you see me slam a family-size bag of Calbee's barbecue chips and a 12-pack of Kirin Lager. But anyway, at least they're subtle about it, which I appreciate.

7. Japanese leisure activities. Singing karaoke till 4 a.m. and then sleeping in the booth until dawn. Floating in a bath under the stars at an outdoor hot spring, surrounded by creepy naked men. Sleeping in Starbucks and nobody bothers you. Passing out after a festival on the grass. Okay, I like to sleep a lot. It keeps my cheeks plump and rosy. And the department store free samples, arcade photo booths, batting cages, all that stuff. Okay, I've never actually been to a batting cage, but it seems kind of fun, what with the flying baseballs and all. So

maybe this weekend.

8. Convenience. Convenience stores on every corner. Color printers and fax machines in convenience stores. A vending machine at the top of a mountain when I'm out for a hike. Taxis everywhere. Underwear in Family Mart for those nights you slept in a karaoke booth and then went straight to work. Taxi doors that open automatically. Toilets that flush automatically and partitions that go all the way to the ground. All that adds up to time and energy saved that I can then use for other things, like, well, drinking beer. Man, I really gotta get a new hobby. Hey, I tried wine and look how well that worked out, so I guess it's back to *shochu*.

9. All the little things. Taking off shoes indoors. Buying fresh vegetables outdoors. Not fearing for my life when I take a couple hundred bucks out of the ATM at night. The city workers who pick up cigarette butts and discarded cans of coffee and cut the limbs off the trees every November before the autumn leaves can litter the ground. Eating pasta with chopsticks.

Well of course I figured I'd write The 10 Best Things About Japan, but when I came back from McDonalds I got so busy dragging my new carpet onto the balcony and trying to de-wineglassify it that I got stuck at nine. Sorry, workplace hazard. And then when I put on the little balcony slippers I could kind of imagine they were ruby-colored, even though they're in fact a faded periwinkle, but still I thought maybe I'd try saying "There's no place like home" a few times just to see what happened.

Well, freaking nothing. No Auntie Em, Uncle Henry, or even a little dog. Still, never hurts to try. I sure would like a dog. But when I said it, I realized, Hmm, yeah, there really is no place. No place like home anymore, and that was kind of strange and a bit nostalgic. Although maybe the incantation actually worked, because I had another moment of clarity. Probably shouldn't have eaten those three hash browns, now that I think about it. Anyway, the clarity said, Well, Seeroi, you're not in Kansas anymore. In fact, you've never even been to Kansas. And hell, you're certainly not in Oz anymore. What you are is a tall white guy in satiny underwear and little blue slippers flapping a big red carpet off a balcony, somewhere in the middle of Japan. And then I realized how fortunate I am to have a balcony that gets such good sunlight, and that made me kind of happy.

Learn Japanese in Five Minutes

arigatou, arigatou gozaimasu	Equivalent to the English "thanks" and "thank you," respectively.
bento	Packaged lunch boxes with rice and an assortment of fish, meat, egg, and vegetables. *Bento* can be purchased in stores or prepared at home.
chikan	Pervert, groper. Most commonly, men who feel up women on trains and busses.
chu-hi	*Shochu* mixed with fruit juice or fruit-flavored soda. Sold in cans in convenience stores, and in mugs at bars and *izakaya*.
daijyoubu	Often translated as "okay," this word literally means "yes" and "no" at the same time. If somebody asks, "Are you okay?" and you reply "*daijyoubu*," it means "yes." If they ask, "Do you want more rice?" and you answer "*daijyoubu*," it means "no." And that, in a nutshell, is the Japanese language.
dame	A very strong "no." No way.
-desu	You can pretend to be polite by ending sentences with this, and Japanese people will pretend to think you are, while secretly knowing your Japanese sucks.
eikaiwa	An English-language conversation school. *Eikaiwa* emphasize spoken communication and minimize grammar, which is exactly opposite to the formal school instruction all Japanese students are forced to endure.
en, yen	The unit of Japanese money. One *en* equals approximately one cent in U.S. currency. Depending upon the preceding word, pronounced either *en* or *yen*.
fugu	A species of pufferfish containing a deadly neurotoxin that, if not prepared perfectly, results in death. Despite being utterly bland and potentially deadly, Japanese people love to eat it so they can say, See, *we* can eat

237

	fugu.
furigana	Small characters written above *kanji* to assist in reading the unreadable. *Furigana* enable you to "sound out" words that appear to have been written by a chicken.
futon	A thin, uncomfortable mattress, typically laid on the floor.
gaijin, gaikokujin	A foreigner. For further details, consult a mirror.
ganbatte	Do your best. Try hard. Don't give up. This is said a lot.
hanami	Flower viewing. Often refers to the massive festivals held under blooming *sakura* trees in the springtime.
hostess club	A lounge featuring young women with big hair who pour drinks and converse with you for exorbitant amounts of money. People who do not appear traditionally Japanese are often denied entry.
irrashaimasei	Welcome. Store clerks and waitstaff are required to say this word all day long. Don't mistake this for them being glad to see you.
itadakimasu	A polite phrase mumbled before starting a meal, particularly when eating at someone's home.
Iyaaa, iyada	An expression of dislike or distaste, similar to the English "eeeew" or "yuck."
izakaya	A Japanese restaurant. This term is often translated as "pub," although that's not really accurate. It's just a restaurant.
jyouzu, umai, pera pera	Words used to describe the language ability of people who don't appear "Japanese." In order, these mean "great," "really great," and "fluent." If you can manage a *konnichiwa*, expect to hear them.
kanji	The Japanese writing system, based upon Chinese characters. Used to prevent Japan from joining the rest of civilization.
kanpai	Cheers. You'll probably say this a lot. At least, I do.
katsuobushi	Dried, shaved bonito. Looks and tastes

	exactly like fish food, only less salty.
konnichiwa	Hello.
mamachari	A mother's chariot, i.e., a basket bike. Sturdy and practical, *mamachari* are ridden by men and women from all walks of life.
mochi	White rice pounded to death with a big wooden mallet, until it becomes a massive gummy mess. Served grilled and in soups, and responsible for several choking deaths per year.
monjyayaki	An insanely watery, savory pancake you grill on a hotplate at your table. *Monjyayaki* looks exactly like somebody just lost their lunch in front of you.
muri	No way.
nama	Literally, "fresh" or "raw." Can refer to a draft beer or sex without a condom.
natto	Fermented soybeans, and the stickiest substance in the universe. *Natto* enjoys a reputation among Japanese folks as a weird food, completely oblivious to the fact that all Japanese foods are weird.
nomihoudai	A restaurant plan offering all-you-can-drink for a set price. From an economic perspective, this is a great deal. From the standpoint of health, eh, not so much.
oden	A bizarre combination of stuff floating in a hot broth, including potatoes, eggs, fish cakes, fried tofu, and daikon radish. Sold at *yatai* and in most convenience stores.
ojisan	A middle-aged man, or uncle. Not to be confused with *ojiisan*, which refers to an elderly man or grandfather.
onigiri	A rice ball. That is, a squished up handful of rice, usually stuffed with a small bit of fish, meat, or vegetable, and often wrapped in seaweed. Sold in convenience stores throughout the nation.
onsen	A mineral hot spring enjoyed as a naked communal bath, typically gender separated.
osechi, osechi-	Traditional foods eaten on New Year's Day,

ryouri	many of which are not great. *Osechi-ryouri* is sold by department stores in stacked lacquer boxes for unreasonable prices.
sake	Rice wine. The recommended Japanese approach for not remembering what happened the night before.
sakura	Cherry blossom trees, found throughout Japan, that bloom with pink flower petals.
-san	A polite name suffix, equivalent to "Mr." or "Ms."
sayonara	Goodbye. This has a rather formal connotation, and is rarely used among friends.
senbero	The semi-literal translation would be "get drunk for a thousand-yen." Bars and izakaya with *senbero* specials typically serve 3 drinks and a small appetizer for 1,000 yen (roughly $10 US).
sensei	An honorific title, typically used for doctors and teachers.
seppuku	A method of ritual suicide performed by plunging a knife into one's abdomen. That this is even a thing should tell you something about Japanese people.
shiso	The green, or occasionally red, leaves of the *shiso* plant, which taste something like a delicious cross between mint and basil.
shochu	A neutral-grain spirit, normally made from potatoes or wheat, like a weak vodka.
shokudo	A low-cost restaurant or cafeteria that sells set meals known as *teishoku*.
snack bar	A bar. You will be served snacks by a middle-aged woman, forced to engage in conversation, and prodded into singing karaoke.
soapland	A brothel with bathtubs. People who look "non-Japanese" are frequently denied entry.
sukiyaki	A boiling cauldron of sliced beef, onions, shitake mushrooms, tofu, and other stuff in a slightly sweet, soy sauce-flavored broth.
sugoi	An exclamation meaning "amazing" or

	"wow." Used in response to the most banal of events. In American English, this would be "awesome."
sumimasen	Literally, "excuse me." Used for both apologies and to call wait staff.
tanuki	A weird-looking animal with a long snout, like a cross between a racoon and a dog. Depicted in Japanese cartoons and statues with absolutely enormous testicles.
tenga	The brand name for a male masturbatory device sold in drug stores throughout Japan. A pocket pussy.
ume, umeboshi	Japanese plums. When pickled with salt, they're known as *umeboshi*. Whoever dreamed this up was a madman, but they taste pretty good.
yakitori	Grilled chicken served on skewers and flavored with salt or sauce. The national dish of Japan.
yakuza	Often referred to as gangsters, although the term is largely overblown. There are various *yakuza* groups throughout the nation, which function similarly to labor unions. Members are typically working-class individuals employed in construction, road work, nightclubs, illegal money lending, and the sex industry.
yatai	An outdoor food stall, sometimes with stools for customer seating. *Yatai* typically serve cheap food, such as ramen or *yakitori*. When crowded, there may be a time limit, and you may be asked to leave.
yoroshiku onegaishimasu	A phrase theoretically implying mutual respect between two parties. In practice, however, it often carries the connotation of "I know this sucks, but do it anyway."
yukata	A light robe, often worn at *onsen* and outdoors during summertime festivals.
zou	Elephant. King of the jungle.

Made in the USA
Monee, IL
14 November 2021